College and the Learning Disabled Student

College and the Learning Disabled Student

A Guide to Program Selection, Development, and Implementation

Charles T. Mangrum II, Ed.D.

Professor of Educational Psychology
Chairman, Graduate Reading Program
University of Miami
Coral Gables, Florida

Stephen S. Strichart, Ph.D.

Professor of Learning Disabilities
Coordinator, Special Education Program
Florida International University
Miami, Florida

Grune & Stratton, Inc.
(Harcourt Brace Jovanovich, Publishers)
Orlando   San Diego   San Francisco
New York   London   Toronto   Montreal
Sydney   Tokyo   São Paulo

Library of Congress Cataloging in Publication Data

Strichart, Stephen S.
    College and the learning disabled student.

    Bibliography: p.
    Includes index.
        1. Physically handicapped—United States—Education
(Higher)   I. Mangrum, Charles T.   II. Title.   [DNLM:
1. Learning disorders.   2. Education, Special.   3. Univer-
sities.   LC   4704   S916c]
LC4820.S77   1984   371.91   83-26368
ISBN   0-8089-1629-7

Grune & Stratton, Inc.
Orlando, FL   32887

Distributed in the United Kingdom by
Grune & Stratton, Ltd.
24/28 Oval Road, London NW 1

Library of Congress Catalog Number 83-26368
International Standard Book Number 0-8089-1629-7
Printed in the United States of America

This book is dedicated to those students who struggle to succeed despite their learning disabilities; to their parents, who give encouragement and support to their learning disabled children; to the professionals who search for ways to help learning disabled students reach their potential; and to the members of organizations who work on behalf of the learning disabled to bring about changes in society and government so that the learning disabled can find a place from which to contribute to the world.

Contents

Preface

How do you advise learning disabled high school students who are concerned about their future? This is a question we have faced increasingly over the past few years. We worked with learning disabled adolescents and young adults who had the desire and potential to continue their academic studies, but who were at a loss as to where to study. Only through many telephone calls and letters did we realize that scattered throughout the nation are colleges that not only are willing to accept learning disabled students, but some that had gone to the extent of designing programs for them. It became clear to us that college opportunities for learning disabled students exist.

To learn more about the opportunities available for learning disabled students, we engaged in a number of activities. We first obtained directories of college learning disabilities programs. After reviewing these, we sent questionnaires to directors of programs listed in these directories. We asked them for information about their program, program design, and policies. Once we identified programs that we believed to be comprehensive, we visited the colleges where these programs are located (see Appendix 1). On these visits, we met with program directors, staff, admission office personnel, and the students participating in the learning disabilities program. In some cases, we communicated with directors of college learning disability programs by telephone and/or through letters. In all of our contacts, we requested that directors of programs respond to the following questions: What are your admission procedures? How would you describe your learning disabilities college program? What are the characteristics of the students in your program? How have you been able to make the program work? Based on your experience, what suggestions do you have for high school personnel to help them better prepare learning disabled students for college?

In addition to these procedures, we conducted a standard literature search including a search via the ERIC service. We used all this information, along with our experience in working with learning disabled high school students and as college professors, to prepare this book.

We describe the factors that have brought college programs for learning disabled students into existence, what college learning disabled students are like, how to develop a college program for learning disabled students, admission procedures, the range of services provided by programs, suggestions for preparing learning disabled high school students for college, suggestions for teaching learning disabled students in college classrooms, and guidelines for selecting programs. At the end of this book, we present an array of resource materials to assist learning disabled students, parents, professionals who work with them, and college personnel in their efforts to make college opportunities for the learning disabled a reality.

There are five important things to keep in mind when reading this book. First, this book is about comprehensive programs that provide a range of services to learning disabled students from the time they enter college. In some cases, services are made available to students after they begin to experience difficulty in college. Second, college learning disabilities programs are designed for students with average or higher intelligence. It is important to realize that college is not an appropriate option for all learning disabled students. Third, colleges with learning disabilities programs do not lower their standards for learning disabled students. These students must meet the same academic requirements as their non–learning-disabled peers. Fourth, students who participate in college learning disabilities programs may work toward any college major or in any college program. Fifth, college learning disabilities programs provide an array of intensive services to students that are designed to allow the students to function independently in college within one or two years.

We could not have written this book without the help of professionals of the highest order. The following professionals shared their ideas and their programs to make this book possible; they are making the world a better place for learning disabled college students: Jeffrey Barsch, Ventura College; Katherine Chandler, Erskine College; Barbara Cordoni, Southern Illinois University; Ignacio Götz, Hofstra University; Joan McGuire, Mitchell College; Robert Nash, University of Wisconsin–Oshkosh; Paul Quinlan, American International College; Doug Saddler, College of the Ozarks; Jeffrey Vernooy, Wright State University; Susan Vogel, Barat College; and Gertrude Webb, Curry College.

Stephen S. Strichart
Charles T. Mangrum

College and the Learning Disabled Student

Pg. 133 – 158 – 160 .

83 – 85

1

The Emergence of College Programs
for Learning Disabled Students

Learning disabilities is a relatively new term that is used as a label for a variety of difficulties people have with learning. The term was introduced in the early 1960s by William Cruickshank and his colleagues (1961) and by Samuel Kirk (1962). These outstanding educators recognized this new category of disabilities and brought it to the attention of educators, psychologists and parents.

In 1963, the first organization to focus its attention exclusively upon learning disabilities was founded. It was called the Association for Children With Learning Disabilities and is often referred to by its initials ACLD. This professional association was founded by parents, educators, psychologists, and other individuals concerned with learning disabilities. Initially, the organization focused upon children, and in 1979 was renamed to show its additional focus upon adults. Today, while maintaining the initials ACLD, it is known as the Association for Children and Adults With Learning Disabilities.

Six years after ACLD was founded, the first federal legislation was passed and funds became available to educate learning disabled children. In 1969, Congress passed Public Law 91-230, which is known as the Children With Specific Learning Disabilities Act. It was this act that provided public schools with funds to hire learning disability teachers and to establish programs to deal with the special problems of learning disabled children.

It was not until the early 1970s that the need for providing college programs for learning disabled students was recognized. Gertrude Webb (1974) at Curry College in Milton, Massachusetts, was one of the first to recognize that many learning disabled students had the ability and desire to go to college and deserved the same opportunity to do so as their non–learning-disabled peers. She also recognized that, for learning

1

disabled students to be successful in college, they needed services beyond those provided by colleges for non–learning-disabled students. Webb developed the Program of Assistance in Learning (PAL) at Curry College to assist capable learning disabled students to enter and succeed in college. Since her pioneer efforts, other colleges and universities have launched similar programs. (See Appendix 2 for directories listing these.)

FACTORS CAUSING COLLEGES AND UNIVERSITIES TO DEVELOP PROGRAMS FOR LEARNING DISABLED STUDENTS

There are at least ten factors that are contributing to the emergence of college programs for learning disabled students. The importance of each factor varies from college to college and university to university but all are contributing to new and better programs for college students with learning disabilities.

Extension of High School Programs

During the 1960s, it was commonly believed that if learning disabled children could be identified and treated early they could be cured of their learning disabilities. This optimism was not fulfilled and it soon became obvious that learning disabilities persist even into adulthood. The result was that elementary school programs were extended to the junior high school and eventually the senior high school levels.

A considerable number of learning disabled students graduate from high school each year. For example, J. Rosenstein, in a personal communication with the authors on March 11, 1983, stated that during the 1981 to 1982 school year, there were 49,965 students classified as learning disabled between the ages of 18 and 21 in the United States. Many of these students graduated from high school and were qualified to go to college. But to be successful in college, the types of support programs they had for their learning disabilities had to be extended into colleges and universities.

Realization that College is a Viable Goal

The basic philosophic premise that learning disabled students can succeed academically if given appropriate programming and adequate support is as applicable to postsecondary education as it is to preceding levels. The learning disabled have the same desire and drive to grow and develop as do the non–learning-disabled. Their desire to obtain more knowledge and prepare for successful careers is not incompatible with having a learning disability. Once the learning disabled, their parents, and professionals who work with them realized that college was a viable goal, pressure was brought upon colleges and universities to offer programs for learning disabled students.

betweehandakkon

Desire of Learning Disabled Students to go to College

Many learning disabled students are interested in going to college. A recent survey reported that 67 percent of young adults who were diagnosed as learning disabled while in elementary or secondary school had plans for future education (White, Alley, Deshler, Schumaker, Warner, & Clark, 1982). While not all learning disabled students who express an interest in continuing their education beyond high school will actually enter college, an increasing number are pursuing this goal. This has brought pressure on colleges and universities to develop programs for them.

Lack of Programs

An examination of recently appearing directories of college programs for learning disabled students suggests that these programs exist in some abundance. A list of these directories appears in Appendix 2. Our analysis of the programs listed in these directories shows that many do not actually provide a program for students with learning disabilities. Programs for learning disabled students must have special admissions procedures, provide specially designed services, and hire staff trained to work with learning disabled students. The components of college programs for learning disabled students are described in Chapters 6 through 13 of this book.

While many colleges and universities claim that they have programs for learning disabled students, they do little more than admit learning disabled students and make their regular support services accessible to them. While the support services typically found in a college or university are very helpful for the regular student, they generally lack the individualization, intensity, regularity, and coordination required to help learning disabled students succeed in college. While the professionals who staff the special services are well trained and competent, they frequently are not trained to work with learning disabled students.

In our work, we have found an insufficient number of college programs designed to specifically and comprehensively meet the needs of learning disabled students. Those programs that do provide for the specialized needs of learning disabled students report long waiting lists of learning disabled applicants. The need for programs is apparent and is a factor that is bringing more programs into being.

The Need to Service Disabled Students
Who Are Attending College

Although definitive data is lacking, there are indications that many learning disabled students are attending colleges and universities. In many cases, they are attending a college where no special program exists to meet their needs. Since applicants to colleges are not required to indicate whether they have a learning disability (see Chapter 2 for a detailed discussion of this point), their presence at the college is generally unknown to college officials.

Rogan and Hartman (1976) studied the adult attainments of 91 children with learning disabilities who received remedial education in a private school. They found that 69 percent had graduated from high school, 36 percent of the subjects in this longitudinal study had completed college, and 8 percent had completed or were pursuing graduate study. At the time of the study, 16 percent were in college. ✓

Further evidence that learning disabled individuals are attending college comes from the Vocational Committee Survey of the Association for Children and Adults with Learning Disabilities (1982). A questionnaire was completed by 562 learning disabled adults. It was found that 14 percent had tried a two-year or four-year college and had dropped out, 32 percent were currently in college, 4 percent had graduated from a junior college, 9 percent had earned a bachelor's degree, and 8 percent had earned or were earning a postgraduate degree.

Data from a much larger sample base was reported by Lawrence, Kent, and Henson (1981). Their report was based on the weighted responses of more than 5000 disabled college freshmen who, when they entered college as first-time, fulltime students in 1978, completed the Student Information Form (SIF). This form has been used since 1965 by the Cooperative Institutional Research Program to survey the entire entering freshman classes of a representative sample of the nation's colleges and universities.

The disabled freshmen were self-identified on the basis of their responses to two items that first appeared on the SIF in 1978. The first item (24a) asked, "Do you consider yourself physically handicapped?" The second item (24b) asked, "If yes, what type of handicap do you have (mark all that apply)?" (Lawrence, et al., 1981, p. 410). The SIF listed the following disability areas: hearing, speech, orthopedic, visual, learning, and other. Respondents who answered "yes" to 24a and/or listed a disability in 24b were counted as disabled. A total of 5401 of the 187,603 college freshmen completing the SIF were identified as disabled (2.9 percent). Of the disabled freshman group, 3.1 percent were classified as learning disabled. Weighted projections indicated that a total of 50,797 disabled students entered college as freshmen in 1978. This would mean that 1575 learning disabled students entered college in 1978. By 1980, the percentage of disabled college freshmen with learning disabilities had risen to 5.6 percent. (Henson, Kent, & Richardson, 1981). Data for 1982 showed that 5.4 percent of entering freshmen were disabled. Of this group, 6.0 percent were learning disabled. (Astin, Hemond, & Richardson, 1982).

It is probable that these data reflect an extremely conservative estimate of the number of learning disabled students entering college each year. The term "physically handicapped" used to self-identify disabled freshmen would result in a much lower than actual figure. While learning disabled students consider themselves to have deficits in learning and social skills, few think of themselves as having a physical handicap. We speculate that many learning disabled college freshmen answered "no" to item 24a and then simply went right past item 24b. They were thus not counted as disabled, accounting for the low percentage of disabled college freshmen who were classified as learning disabled. In the same communication on March 11, 1983, Rosenstein informed us that 38.4 percent of all handicapped students in the public schools in 1981 to 1982 were classified as learning disabled. The total number of learning disabled students ages 3 through 21 years was 1,627,362. These data further indicate that the number of learning disabled students reported as entering college in the last several years has been greatly underestimated.

Because many learning disabled students are attending colleges and universities that do not have programs designed for them, an increasing number of these institutions are developing methods to identify learning disabled students already on campus. Knowles and Knowles (1983) found that by using the American College Test (ACT), the reading section of the Stanford Test of Academic Skills (TASK), and the high school gradepoint average (GPA) of incoming college freshmen, learning disabled students could be identified with 84 percent accuracy. Such predictive techniques will enable more and more institutions to identify learning disabled students and provide programs for them.

The Effect of Open Enrollment

The movement toward open enrollment admission policies at colleges and universities has resulted in many students pursuing higher education who previously would have been hesitant to apply in expectation of being denied admission. The open enrollment phenomenon is particularly significant at the community college level. As more learning disabled students enroll in institutions through open admission policies, and become known to college officials because of their special needs, more programs for learning disabled college students will emerge. Chapter 5 of this handbook fully describes admission policies that affect learning disabled students.

Pressure from Advocates

Vogel (1982) observed that colleges, universities, and graduate and professional schools are responding to the powerful pressure of the community of concerned learning disabled adolescents, their parents, learning disabled adults, and professionals. Progress in providing educational services for the handicapped historically has been brought about by nonprofessional and professional advocates who have organized their efforts through various associations. This is happening on behalf of the young learning disabled adult as evidenced by the formation of a number of adult oriented groups consisting of learning disabled individuals and their advocates, such as the following organizations:

Association of Learning Disabled Adults
Georgia Association for Adults with Learning Disabilities
Launch, Inc.
Learning Disabled Adult Committee of the Association for Children and
    Adults with Learning Disabilities (ACLD)
National Network of Learning Disabled Adults
Pennsylvania Youth and Adult Organization
Time Out to Enjoy, Inc.
The Puzzle People

Appendix 3 contains a list of names and addresses of associations and organizations providing services and information to learning disabled adolescents and adults.

Source of Enrollment and Revenue

Colleges and universities are facing serious financial crises due to a leveling off of student enrollments and increasing operational costs. Edles (1981) observed that after peaking in 1981, enrollments in higher education are expected to taper off through the decade, reflecting the declining birth rate of the 1960s. College enrollment, which reached a total of 12.1 million in 1981 (*Women Are Increasing...*, 1983) is projected to drop to 11 million by 1988 (Anderson, 1981).

Enrollment projections are extremely important since the key to the financial health of many colleges and universities is tied to enrollments (Leslie, 1982). While enrollments are not expected to increase, the cost of operating colleges and universities is. The total expenditure of institutions of higher education rose from approximately 36 billion dollars in 1974 to 1975 to almost 51 billion dollars in 1978 to 1979 (Anderson, 1981). This is a 29 percent increase in instructional costs during a four-year period.

These circumstances suggest that colleges and universities will be looking for new sources of student enrollments. Fielding (1981) claims that over 16 million adults with learning disabilities are potential consumers of postsecondary educational services. He characterizes this group as constituting the largest pool of undereducated and underemployed but high potential persons in our nation today. It is his belief that institutions with foresight and willingness to serve this population will find a ready and capable group. It is our belief that many institutions of higher learning will come to this realization in the very near future.

Philosophical Commitment

Fred Barbaro, Director of the Program for Learning Disabled College Students at Adelphi University, has raised an important philosophical issue (Barbaro, 1982). He comments that college and university officials often speak about the social mission of their institutions in grant proposals, in promotional materials, and at commencement exercises and, therefore, must be committed to do all they can to provide opportunities for academic and social success for learning disabled students. This commitment to the social mission will make college possibilities for the learning disabled a reality.

Special Education Legislation

The greatest force behind the movement to provide college programs for learning disabled students has been the passage of strong legislation at the state and federal levels. Because of the important effects that legislation has had upon college programs for learning disabled students, this legislation will be discussed in detail in the next chapter.

Lawrence, Kent, and Henson (1982) revealed the significance of providing college opportunities for qualified learning disabled students when they concluded on the basis of their follow-up of 1978 disabled college freshmen that the majority of respondents to their 1983 questionnaire had done well in college. As they stated, "Give the disabled access to colleges and universities, and they will match the nondisabled in their performance, progress, and promise," (Lawrence, et al., 1982, p. 164).

2

The Impact of Federal and State Laws

To understand the impact of the law upon college programs for learning disabled students, one must know about three laws. The first is a federal law known as Public Law 94-142 (PL 94-142). It was signed into law in 1975, and implementing regulations appeared in the August 23, 1977 issue of the *Federal Register*. The second is a California state law known as Assembly Bill No. 77 (AB-77). This bill was passed by the California legislature in 1976. The last is another federal law known as Public Law 93-112 (PL 93-112), titled, The Rehabilitation Act of 1973. Section 504 of this Act bears directly upon college programs for learning disabled students. Final regulations for Section 504 appeared in the *Federal Register*, May 4, 1977.

The least restrictive environment stipulation of PL 94-142 requires that handicapped children between the ages of 3 and 21 years be educated in regular class settings with nonhandicapped children to the greatest appropriate extent. This has meant that increasing numbers of learning disabled high school students attend regular classes with non–learning-disabled students. As they do so, many acquire the same aspirations for college as their non–learning-disabled peers.

AB-77 was passed to ensure provision of appropriate services to handicapped students enrolled in community colleges throughout California who could not benefit from the regular educational program provided by these colleges. Since PL 94-142 applies only to students through secondary school, AB-77 is important because it extends similar provisions into the postsecondary level in California and we believe many other states will soon follow their lead.

Section 504 of the Rehabilitation Act of 1973 (PL 93-112) requires that no qualified handicapped person, on the basis of handicap, be discriminated against in any program or activity receiving federal financial assistance. Since the federal government defines financial assistance to include veteran's education benefits and other student financial aid programs such as the Basic and Supplemental Educational Opportunity Grant Programs and the Guaranteed Student Loan Program, it is very unlikely that any college or university would be able to argue successfully that it is not covered by Section 504 (Guthrie, 1979).

In the case of each of these laws, the learning disabled fall within the definition of handicapped individuals. Because PL 94-142 does not directly apply beyond the secondary level, it will not be discussed in detail in this book. Components of AB-77 and Section 504 are presented in detail, and their implications discussed.

AB-77   *Klst un Exam*

AB-77 was signed into law on June 26, 1976, and was filed as Chapter 275 in the California Education Code. The Board of Governors of the California Community Colleges adopted regulations implementing this bill on February 25, 1977. Within the regulations, learning disability is defined in considerable detail as follows:

Learning disability refers to students with exceptional learning needs who have neurological, biochemical or developmental limitations. These limitations result from atypical perception, cognition or response to environmental stimuli, manifested by inadequate ability to manipulate educational symbols in an expected manner. Typical limitations include inadequate ability to listen, speak, read, write, spell, concentrate, remember or do computation. These students demonstrate a significant discrepancy between their achievement and potential levels because of one or more of the following:

(a) *Neurological Limitation* refers to the exceptional learning needs of a student with average academic potential. Their learning needs are a result of genetic aberrations, disease, birth complications, traumatic brain insult, or poor nutrition. These conditions may range from mild to severe and are associated with deviations of the function of the central nervous system.

(b) *Biochemical Limitation* refers to the exceptional learning needs of a student with average academic potential. Their learning needs are a result of excesses or depletions of hormonal, neurochemical or metabolic substances associated with diminished motoric, perceptual or cognitive capabilities.

(c) *Developmental Limitation* refers to:

(1) The exceptional learning needs of a student with average academic potential. Their learning needs are a result of delayed educational development, incurred through maturational delays and/or any combination of limitations described in subsections (a) or (b) above.

(2) Exceptional learning needs of a student who has limited learning potential, with substantial and/or severe functional limitations and whose limitations can be expected to continue indefinitely. (AB-77, Section 56024, 1976, material in public domain)

The provisions of AB-77 are far ranging and powerful. AB-77 ensures that learning disabled students will have fair opportunity to fully participate in all that California community colleges have to offer to students. Important components of AB-77 follow.

Support Services and Programs

Support services and programs are designed to enable handicapped students to participate in the regular activities, programs and classes offered by the college (Sections 56002, 56030). These are services that are in addition to the regular services provided to all students and may include, but need not be limited to: specific purpose counseling; special registration assistance; college orientation; specific assessment for academic, career, or vocational planning and placement; special facilities; special educational materials; mobility, housing and transportation assistance; developing and maintaining attendant, reader, and interpreter rosters; on-campus aides; equipment loan repair; and other services appropriate to the students' particular needs.

Participation

Participation by a student in any supportive services or programs shall not preclude participation in any other service or program that may be offered by the college. Further, participation in any aspect of the supportive services program shall be voluntary. Each Community College district is required to use reasonable means to inform the general college population as to the availability of supportive services and programs (Section 56004).

Student Rights

No program or course shall be denied a student without due consideration of the student's potential and abilities, and of the additional assistance provided by adaptive or sensory aids or other supportive services or programs (Section 56006).

Program Placement and
Individualized Educational Planning

Assessment of the student's educational competency and needs shall be made by appropriately certified, licensed, or credentialed special instructor(s) in conjunction with the student, other appropriate college staff, professional persons from the community, or other agencies that are working with the student. If requested by the student, all prescriptive, individualized plans shall be reviewed and amended as needed each semester or quarter by designated specialists working with the student. Each individual educational plan must specifically include (Section 56060):

1. The academic and career assessment tools, if any, utilized to identify the competency level of the student upon enrollment.
2. A clear description of the courses, programs or activities a student will engage in to improve academic or career competency.
3. Functional recommendations for the use of appropriate instructional materials and equipment.
4. A clear description of monitoring devices or procedures that assess improvement of compentency based on the education program design being implemented.
5. Evidence of measurable improvement at the conclusion of each semester in which the student is enrolled.

The impact of AB-77 has been significant in California. Ostertag, Baker, Howard, and Best (1982) surveyed the 106 California community colleges and found that 80 colleges (75.4 percent) operated formal programs for the learning disabled, while an additional 13 (12 percent) provided informal services for their learning disabled student population. Learning disabled students were receiving a range of comprehensive services including tutoring, remediation, counseling, arrangement for reproduction of lectures, modification of class schedules, revisions of course curricula, extended time to complete course requirements, waiver or extended time to complete degree requirements, course substitutions, and a number of auxiliary support services (reader, notetaker, registration assistance, diagnostic learning assessment).

It seems likely to us that other states will follow the lead of California and provide special services to assist learning disabled students to succeed in community colleges. We believe, further, that similar provisions will be extended to four year colleges and universities in the near future.

SECTION 504

Many people are surprised to learn that Section 504 of the Rehabilitation Act of 1973 (PL 93-112) is only one sentence long. Here is the law.

No otherwise qualified handicapped individual in the United States, shall solely by reason of his handicap, be excluded from participation in, be denied the benefits of, or be subjected to discrimination under any program or activity receiving Federal financial assistance. (PL 93-112, 1973, material in public domain)

Once this law was passed by Congress, it became the responsibility of the Department of Health, Education and Welfare (HEW) to write implementing regulations. Following the process of publishing initial regulations and inviting public comments in response, final regulations for Section 504 appeared in 1977. The regulations provided specific details for putting the law into practice. An accompanying analysis by HEW staff responded to various comments and provided additional interpretation and elaboration of the law.

Section 504 defines a handicapped person as any person who has a physical or mental impairment that substantially limits one or more major life activity. Specific learning disability is listed as one such impairment. Learning is considered one of the major life activities.

The regulations of May 4, 1977, have vast importance for college learning disabilities programs. The requirement that colleges receiving any federal financial assistance be in compliance with the Section 504 regulations has been a major factor in spurring more institutions to admit qualified learning disabled students and provide appropriate services for them. The ways in which colleges are to accomplish this is addressed by Subpart E of Section 504. Subpart E refers specifically to postsecondary education.

A qualified handicapped person is defined as one who meets the academic and technical standards requisite to admission or participation in an education program or activity. Guthrie (1979) feels that when read as a whole, Section 504 appears to regard a "qualified" handicapped applicant or student as a handicapped person who, with an auxiliary aid or reasonable program modification, can meet the academic requirements that an institution can demonstrate are essential to its education program.

Subpart E of Section 504 requires that qualified handicapped persons be provided aids, benefits, and services that are as effective as those afforded others. This does not mean that these aids, benefits, and services must produce the identical result or level of achievement for handicapped and nonhandicapped persons, but rather, must afford handicapped persons equal opportunity to obtain the same result, to gain the same benefit, or to reach the same level of achievement. This is to be done in the most integrated setting appropriate to the qualified handicapped person's needs.

Where a recipient of federal funding is found to be in violation of Section 504 because of discrimination against persons on the basis of their handicap, they may be required to take remedial action. A recipient may take voluntary action to overcome the effects of conditions that have resulted in limited participation in their program or activity by qualified handicapped persons.

Subpart E clearly prohibits discrimination against qualified handicapped persons in admissions, recruitment, and treatment after admission. Because of its importance, we present Subpart E in its entirety. After each section, we provide an interpretation.

Section 84.42. Admissions and Recruitment

(a) *General.* Qualified handicapped persons may not, on the basis of handicap, be denied admission or be subjected to discrimination in admission or recruitment by a recipient to which this Subpart applies.

(b) *Admissions.* In administering its admission policies, a recipient to which this Subpart applies:

(1) may not apply limitations upon the number or proportion of handicapped persons who may be admitted;

(2) may not make use of any test or criterion for admission that has a disproportionate, adverse effect on handicapped persons or any class of handicapped persons unless (i) the test or criterion, as used by the recipient, has been validated as a predictor of success in the education program or activity in question and (ii) alternate tests or criteria that have a less disproportionate, adverse effect are not shown by the Director to be available;

(3) shall assure itself that (i) admissions tests are selected and administered so as best to ensure that, when the test is administered to an applicant who has a handicap that impairs sensory, manual, or speaking skills, the test results accurately reflect the applicant's aptitude or achievement level or whatever other factor the test purports to measure, rather than reflecting the applicant's impaired sensory, manual, or speaking skills (except where those skills are factors that the test purports to measure); (ii) admissions tests that are designed for persons with impaired sensory, manual, or speaking skills are offered as often and in as timely a manner as are other admissions tests; and (iii) admissions tests are administered in facilities that, on the whole, are accessible to handicapped persons; and

(4) except as provided in paragraph (c) of this section, may not make preadmission inquiry as to whether an applicant for admission is a handicapped person but, after admission, may make inquiries on a confidential basis as to handicaps that may require accommodation.

(c) *Preadmission inquiry exception.* When a recipient is taking remedial actions to correct the effects of past discrimination or when a recipient is taking voluntary action to overcome the effects of conditions that resulted in limited participation in its federally assisted program or activity, the recipient may invite applicants for admission to indicate whether and to what extent they are handicapped, *Provided,* That:

(1) the recipient states clearly on any written question they use for this purpose and makes clear orally if no written question is used that the

information requested is intended for use solely in connection with its remedial action obligations or its voluntary action efforts; and

(2)   the recipient states clearly that the information is being requested on a voluntary basis, that it will be kept confidential, that refusal to provide it will not subject the applicant to any adverse treatment, and that it will be used only in accordance with this part.

(d)   *Validity studies.*   For the purpose of paragraph (b)(2) of this section, a recipient may base prediction equations on first year grades, but shall conduct periodic validity studies against the criterion of overall success in the education program or activity in question in order to monitor the general validity of the test scores. (PL 93-112, Subpart E, Section 84.42, 1973, material in public domain)

Interpretation of Section 84.42

Recruitment

Because recruitment activities constitute the first contact between a learning disabled student and an institution, Hanson (1979) encourages college administrators to ensure that recruitment materials carry a statement of compliance with Section 504 requirements. She urges that recruiters take accessibility into account in their choice of recruitment sites, that they make clear the ways in which their institution provides special services, and portray accurately the accessibility of their campus and its programs.

Admission Policy

Sedita (1980) notes that handicapped applicants with a High School diploma or its equivalent should be able to gain admission to any postsecondary program that is using an open enrollment policy. She comments that Section 504 appears to have its greatest impact where admission policies use standardized tests and GPA since these may be reflections of a learning disabled applicant's handicap.

Alternative admission policies.   Institutions are permitted to use test scores that may not have the same meaning for handicapped applicants as they do for nonhandicapped applicants, provided they consider other admission factors in making their decisions (Hanson, 1979). As noted by Redden, Levering, and Di Quinzio (1978), institutions are in compliance with Section 504 if in addition to such tests they take other factors into account such as school grades and recommendations. Redden and her colleagues point out that whenever an institution provides information regarding tests required for admission, they must include a statement that special testing arrangements can be made for handicapped applicants. They must further indicate that there are alternate admission criteria for handicapped applicants unable to take the required tests. Both the SAT and the ACT may be taken under special testing conditions. As Sedita (1980) points out, however, scores obtained in special administrations of the SAT and ACT are reported to institutions with a blanket disclaimer of their reliability.

Academic and Technical Standards

Since academic and technical standards vary depending on an institution's policy and programs, a handicapped applicant may be considered qualified by one program and not qualified by another (Ross and O'Brien, 1981). As noted earlier, a qualified handicapped person is one who meets the academic and technical standards requisite to admission or participation in a program. The interpretation of what constitutes academic and technical standards is crucial.

Academic standards are relatively straightforward to interpret. Ross and O'Brien (1981) regard academic standards as those qualifications that indicate an applicant's achievement in academic areas, such as High School records and standardized test results.

Technical standards are more difficult to interpret. In an analysis of the Section 504 regulations by HEW, technical standards were defined as all nonacademic admissions criteria that are essential to participation in a program. Ross and O'Brien (1981) note that while the law does not specifically define essential, it appears to them to refer to those non-academic admission criteria that are absolutely necessary for a student to successfully complete a program of study.

Bailey (1979) points out that in some cases technical standards may have a disproportionate, adverse effect on handicapped applicants, and on that basis may be deemed discriminatory. As an example of such a standard, she cites the requirement of a veterinary school that handicapped applicants demonstrate enough strength and dexterity to lift and handle heavy animals.

Academic and/or technical standards considered by an institution to be essential because they are required by an outside licensing agency are not regarded as discriminatory, even though they may have a negative effect on handicapped applicants. The HEW analysis of the Section 504 regulations clearly shows that the intent of the law is not to allow handicapped individuals access to any program or activity merely because they are handicapped. As revealed in the HEW analysis, it was not Congress's intention that a blind person possessing all of the qualifications for driving a bus except sight be considered qualified for the job of driving.

The interpretation of whether a particular standard is discriminatory is often a cloudy issue. Bailey (1979) cites the example of a prominent medical school that has an entrance requirement of sound eyesight, based largely on the requirement in many states that licensed MDs must have completed training in surgery. One might find this standard discriminatory because it has a disproportionate, adverse effect on blind applicants. On the other hand, it might be interpreted as an acceptable standard because it is based on a directly related licensing requirement.

The Supreme Court decision in Southeastern Community College versus Davis (1978) provides some guidance. In this case the court ruled that the college could refuse to admit a hearing-disabled applicant to its registered nursing program on the ground that the applicant could not participate safely in the program's required clinical training. In this perspective, a qualified handicapped person must be able to meet the requirements of a program in spite of their handicap (assuming reasonable accommodations). Institutions are not expected to alter the basic nature of their program.

Qualified Handicapped Applicant

As stated earlier, a qualified handicapped applicant may be regarded as one who, with an auxiliary aid or reasonable program modification, can meet the academic requirements deemed essential to a program. Vogel (1982) points out an inherent problem with the somewhat vague notion of what constitutes a "qualified" handicapped applicant. She believes that admissions officers, with their limited knowledge of learning disabilities, and the absence of research to guide them, will have great difficulty deciding which learning disabled applicants are qualified and which are not.

Disclosure of Handicap

Vogel (1982) identified another problem for college and university officials. In order to comply with Section 504 in terms of providing services (as described in the next section of this chapter), these officials must know which students are handicapped. They are prohibited, however, from requiring handicapped applicants to make this information known. Vogel observes that in contrast to obvious handicapped conditions such as physical disability or blindness, a learning disability is not apparent. Further, it is her finding that many learning disabled applicants do not divulge the nature of their handicap for fear that it will hurt them in some way. Many learning disabled applicants may consequently go unnoticed and therefore may be denied admission on the basis of their handicap in a nonintentional manner.

The law gives some relief in that an institution may take voluntary action to overcome the effects of past discrimination against the handicapped by inviting preadmission disclosures of a handicap. Redden et al (1978) cautioned that in so doing, the institution must state clearly on any written questionnaire used for this purpose or make clear orally if no written questionnaire is used, that information requested is intended for use solely in connection with the institution's remedial action obligation or its voluntary action efforts; and they must state clearly that the information is being requested on a voluntary basis, that it will be kept confidential, and that refusal of an applicant to provide it will not subject the applicant to any adverse treatment.

Preadmission disclosure of a learning disability by an applicant can be helpful to a college in its efforts to plan and provide appropriate services for that student upon his or her arrival on campus. Where this does not occur, colleges must make every effort to encourage learning disabled students to bring their problem to the attention of directors of appropriate services. This is not a problem in cases in which a college offers a special program for learning disabled students. As discussed in Chapter 5 of this book, admission to these special programs is separate from admission to the college or university, and requires a carefully established diagnosis of a learning disability.

Section 84.43.   Treatment of Students: General

(a)   No qualified handicapped student shall, on the basis of handicap, be excluded from participation in, be denied the benefits of, or otherwise be subjected to discrimination under any academic, research, occupational training, housing, health insurance, counseling, financial aid, physical education, athletics, recreation, transportation, other extracurricula, or other postsecondary education program or activity to which this subpart applies.

(b)   A recipient to which this subpart applies that considers participation by students in education programs or activities not operated wholly by the recipient as part of, or equivalent to, an education program or activity operated by the recipient shall assure itself that the other education program or activity, as a whole, provides an equal opportunity for the participation of qualified handicapped persons.

(c)   A recipient to which this subpart applies may not, on the basis of handicap, exclude any qualified handicapped student from any course, course of study, or any other part of its education program or activity.

(d)   A recipient to which this subpart applies shall operate its program and activities in the most integrated setting appropriate. (PL 93-112, Subpart E, Section 84.43, 1973, material in the public domain)

Interpretation of Section 84.43

This section of Subpart E clearly shows the mainstreaming emphasis of the law. Handicapped students, once admitted, are to be full and active participants in the programs and activities of the institution. This philosophy is consistent with the concept of a qualified handicapped student. Such handicapped individuals are viewed as being able to participate in and benefit from all aspects of the institution's education program or activity. Services to handicapped students are to be provided in the most integrated setting appropriate.

It is important to realize that Section 504 applies to handicapped individuals on a case-by-case basis. Institutions may not treat handicapped students as a class. An example found in the HEW analysis of the regulations makes this clear. There would be a violation if in moving one physics class to the first floor of a building to accommodate students in wheelchairs, a college concentrated handicapped students without mobility impairments in the same class.

Section 84.44.   Academic Adjustments

(a)   *Academic requirements.*   A recipient to which this subpart applies shall make such modifications to its academic requirements as are necessary to ensure that such requirements do not discriminate or have the effect of discriminating, on the basis of handicap, against a qualified handicapped applicant or student. Academic requirements that the recipient can demonstrate are essential to the program of instruction being pursued by such students or to any directly related licensing requirement will not be regarded as discriminatory within the meaning of this section. Modifications may include changes in the length of time permitted for the completion of degree requirements, substitution of specific courses required for the completion of degree requirements, and adaptation of the manner in which specific courses are conducted.

(b)   *Other rules.*   A recipient to which this subpart applies may not impose upon handicapped students other rules, such as the prohibition of tape recorders in classrooms or dog guides in campus buildings, that have the effect of limiting the handicapped students in the recipient's education program or activity.

(c)   *Course examinations.*   In its course examinations or other procedures for evaluating students' academic achievement in its program, the recipient to which this subpart applies shall provide such methods for evaluating the achievement of students who have a handicap that impairs sensory, manual, or speaking skills as will best ensure that the results of the evaluation represents the students' achievement in the course, rather than reflecting the students' impaired sensory, manual, or speaking skills (except where such skills are the factors that the test purports to measure).

(d)   *Auxiliary aids.*

(1)   A recipient to which this subpart applies shall take such steps as are necessary to ensure that no handicapped student is denied the benefits of, excluded from participation in, or otherwise subjected to discrimination under the education program or activity operated by the recipient because of the absence of educational auxiliary aids for students with impaired sensory, manual, or speaking skills.

(2) Auxiliary aids may include taped texts, interpreters or other effective methods of making orally delivered materials available to students with hearing impairments, readers in libraries for students with visual impairments, equipment adapted for use by students with manual impairments, and other similar services and actions. Recipients need not provide attendants, individually prescribed devices, readers for personal use or study, or other devices or services of a personal nature. (PL 93-112, Subpart E, Section 84.44, material in public domain)

Interpretation of Section 84.44

Waiver of Courses or Requirements

In discussing academic requirements and adjustments, Bailey (1979) stated that all parties to the regulatory process (regulators, regulated, and protected class) were in agreement that college curricula should in no case be watered down. Commenting from the perspective of handicapped students, he observed that "The last thing that a handicapped college student wants is a degree that will leave him less qualified than his able-bodied peers," (p. 101). Section 504 does not obligate an institution to waive specific courses or academic requirements. What it does require is that an institution modify its academic requirements as necessary to ensure that they do not discriminate on the basis of handicap. An example found in the HEW analysis is that a college should permit an otherwise qualified student who is deaf to substitute an art appreciation or a music history course for a required course in music appreciation. Another alternative would be to modify the manner in which the music appreciation course is taught for the deaf student.

Institutions are not required to change academic requirements considered essential to a particular program of study or academic degree. The judgment of what is essential is a difficult matter. Jastram (1979) stated that, "there will probably be no more persistent or difficult problem for faculty members than this question of how far it is reasonable or appropriate to go in waiving specific requirements or modifying significant skill-developing exercises in order to accommodate the limitations of a particular handicapped student," (p. 19). Some situations are likely to be relatively clear-cut. For example, we would not expect an art department at a college to modify its requirements so that blind students would not have to critically evaluate art through the visual modality. In point of fact, the law does not define essential. Ross and O'Brien (1981) point out that faculty involved in a program of study must be able to defend their choice of what is regarded as essential for their program. Jastram (1979) presents several examples that are representative of the difficulty in making decisions about essential components:

- Should a physically handicapped student be denied the opportunity to major in astronomy if he or she cannot get to and manipulate a telescope?
- Should a deaf student be precluded from entering a music major because of his or her reliance on visual learning?
- Should a blind student be excluded from English literature or foreign language courses because his or her dependence on a tape recorder makes it difficult for the student to meet normal reading requirements in these courses?

Alternative Examinations

The requirement that institutions make available, where appropriate, alternative course examinations parallels that previously discussed with regard to admission tests. The intent of the law is that course examinations be designed so as to reflect a handicapped student's degree of achievement or ability with respect to certain course material or requirements, rather than simply reflect their handicap. As an obvious example, a blind student's mastery of European history could not be fairly determined by the use of an objective written examination in the standard form. A reasonable adaptation in this situation would be to have someone read the questions to the student and record the student's answers.

Use of Tape Recorders in Class

Some concern has been raised by college faculty about allowing students to tape record their lectures. This is a potential problem when the professor intends to copyright the lecture material. To reduce this concern, colleges might require that students sign an agreement that they will not release the tape recording or transcription or otherwise impede the professor's ability to obtain a copyright.

Cost of Auxiliary Services

Concern has been raised generally with the cost involved in providing auxiliary aids for handicapped students. Auxiliary aids, as referred to in Section 504, include taped texts, interpreters, readers, and adapted classroom equipment. In response to the issue of excessive cost, analysis by HEW indicated that auxiliary aids do not have to be on hand at all times as long as no handicapped student is excluded from a program because of the lack of an appropriate aid. The HEW analysis urged colleges and universities to reduce their costs by utilizing the services of state vocational rehabilitation agencies and private charitable organizations.

Appropriate Modifications

While certain types of modifications are suggested within the regulations for Section 504, there has been no official interpretation of what modifications of academic requirements must be made. When discussing modifications for learning disabled students, Vogel (1982) suggested: modifying or waiving foreign language requirements; allowing for parttime rather than fulltime study; and allowing readers for students taking objective examinations. Sedita (1980) suggested: providing tutors for content courses; providing basic skills tutoring for improving reading, writing, and study skills; implementing a bookless curriculum geared to meet the needs of those students who can learn advanced material but who have reading difficulties; and allowing students who have difficulty taking notes because of writing deficiencies to bring tape recorders to class.

Section 84.45. Housing

(a) *Housing provided by the recipient.* A recipient that provides housing to its nonhandicapped students shall provide comparable, convenient, and accessible housing to handicapped students at the same cost as to others. At the end of the transition period provided for in Subpart C, such housing shall be available in sufficient quantity and variety so that the scope of handicapped students' choice of living accommodations is, as a whole, comparable to that of nonhandicapped students.

(b) *Other housing.* A recipient that assists any agency, organization, or person in making housing available to any of its students shall take such action as may be necessary to assure itself that such housing is, as a whole, made available in a manner that does not result in discrimination on the basis of handicap. (PL 93-112, Subpart E, Section 84.45, material in public domain)

Interpretation of Section 84.45

Hanson (1979) observes that colleges and universities with formal off-campus housing referral services that involve inspection and certification of private housing are not likely to face serious difficulties regarding Section 504 compliance. Where off-campus housing referral services operate less formally (as is most often the case), Hanson suggests that the college or university seek housing lists from disabled consumer groups such as the Disabled Veterans; ask landlords if they have disabled tenants now or have had them in the past; and inspect facilities to ensure that accommodations listed as accessible to the handicapped are in fact accessible.

The transition period referred to in Subpart C of the Section 504 regulations pertains to situations in which structural changes to facilities are necessary. This has little or no relevance for learning disabled students.

Section 84.46. Financial and Employment Assistance to Students

(a) *Provision of financial assistance.*

(1) In providing financial assistance to qualified handicapped persons, a recipient to which this subpart applies may not (i), on the basis of

handicap, provide less assistance than is provided to nonhandicapped persons, limit eligibility for assistance, or otherwise discriminate or (ii) assist any entity or person that provides assistance to any of the recipient's students in a manner that discriminates against qualified handicapped persons on the basis of handicap.

(2) A recipient may administer or assist in the administration of scholarships, fellowships, or other forms of financial assistance established under wills, trusts, bequests, or similar legal instruments that require awards to be made on the basis of factors that discriminate or have the effect of discriminating on the basis of handicap only if the overall effect of the award of scholarships, fellowships, and other forms of financial assistance is not discriminatory on the basis of handicap.

(b) *Assistance in making available outside employment.* A recipient that assists any agency, organization, or person in providing employment opportunities to any of its students shall assure itself that such employment opportunities, as a whole, are made available in a manner that would not violate Subpart B if they were provided by the recipient.

(c) *Employment of students by recipients.* A recipient that employs any of its students may not do so in a manner that violates Subpart B. (PL 93-112, Subpart E, Section 84.46, material in the public domain)

Interpretation of Section 84.46

Common sense must be applied when interpreting this part of the Section 504 regulations. Based on HEW analysis, it would not be considered discriminatory to deny on the basis of handicap, an athletic scholarship to a handicapped person if the handicap renders the person unable to qualify for the award. For example, a student with a neurologic disorder might be denied a varsity football scholarship on the basis of his inability to play football, but a deaf person could not, on the basis of handicap, be denied a scholarship for the school's diving team. The deaf student could, however, be denied a scholarship on the basis of comparative diving ability.

Subpart B of Section 504 applies to employment practices. Once again, the intent of the law is to assure that qualified handicapped individuals are not denied equal opportunities on the basis of their handicap.

Section 84.47.　Nonacademic Services

(a) *Physical education and athletics.*

(1) In providing physical education courses and athletics and similar programs and activities to any of its students, a recipient to which this subpart applies may not discriminate on the basis of handicap. A recipient that offers physical education courses or that operates or sponsors intercollegiate, club, or intramural athletics shall provide to qualified handicapped students an equal opportunity for participation in these activities.

(2)   A recipient may offer to handicapped students physical education and athletic activities that are separate or different only if separation or differentiation is consistent with the requirements of Section 84.43(d) and only if no qualified handicapped student is denied the opportunity to compete for teams or to participate in courses that are not separate or different.

(b)   *Counseling and placement services.*   A recipient to which this subpart applies that provides personal, academic, or vocational counseling, guidance, or placement services to a student shall provide these services without discrimination on the basis of handicap. The recipient shall ensure that qualified handicapped students are not counseled toward more restrictive career objectives than are nonhandicapped students with similar interests and abilities. This requirement does not preclude a recipient from providing factual information about licensing and certification requirements that may present obstacles to handicapped persons in their pursuit of particular careers.

(c)   *Special organizations.*   A recipient that provides significant assistance to fraternities, sororities, or similar organizations shall assure itself that the membership practices of such organizations do not permit discrimination otherwise prohibited by this Subpart. (PL 93-112, Subpart E, Section 84.47, material in public domain)

Interpretation of Section 84.47

The general intent of this part of the Section 504 regulations is to ensure that no qualified handicapped student will be excluded from programs or activities and further, that their needs shall be taken into account in determining the aid, benefits, or services to be provided under a program or activity.

Of particular interest is the stipulation that qualified handicapped students are not to be counseled toward restrictive career objectives. This means in effect that learning disabled students may enroll in a wide variety of college majors. Indeed, this seems to be the case. Barbara Cordoni, director of Project Achieve at Southern Illinois University in Carbondale, has told us that students in her program are in every major from Anthropology to Zoology. Advisement and counseling services provided to learning disabled students in college programs are fully described in Chapters 8 and 13 of this handbook.

As noted earlier in this chapter, the State and Federal legislation described pertains to handicapped students in general. In each case, learning disabled students constitute one specific category of handicapped individuals to whom the legislation pertains. Directly and indirectly these laws have paved the way for and have helped to determine the nature of college programs for learning disabled students. While our treatment of these laws has included their applicability to handicapped students in general, later chapters of this book will explain adjustments, policies, procedures, and services that colleges and universities have made specifically for learning disabled students.

The potential impact of Section 504 is considerable. Its spirit is well characterized by Jastram (1979) when he wrote, "Often the only way to find out whether a student can successfully negotiate a program is for him to try it.... The right to the chance to succeed implies the corresponding right to the chance to fail," (p. 20).

3

Characteristics of Learning
Disabled College Students

Not a great deal is known about the characteristics of those learning disabled students who attend college. Because of the recency of learning disabilities college programs, information about these students is just now beginning to accrue. In this chapter, we present characteristics of learning disabled college students derived from our analysis of various written accounts and our discussions with a number of directors of college learning disabilities programs.

We must make several points about the characteristics we present for learning disabled college students. First, we focused specifically upon characteristics descriptive of students attending learning disabilities college programs. We did not include characteristics reported for learning disabled adults in general, nor those in Adult Basic Education programs. The characteristics we present may, therefore, differ in certain respects from those presented by authors who are describing learning disabled adults in the generic sense (See, for example, Smith, 1983).

Second, most reports of characteristics of learning disabled college students were based upon observation and clinical work and not on empirical research. Very few research studies sought to identify the characteristics of learning disabled college students. Some studies in which researchers were interested in the characteristics of learning disabled adults used college students as subjects, and thus the results shed light on the characteristics of college learning disabled students.

Third, as expected in a field that focuses upon disabilities, most reports were of deficits rather than of strengths. While the characteristics presented are negatively toned, it should be kept in mind that learning disabled college students have many positive attributes.

Finally, all of the characteristics do not apply to any one learning disabled college student. Each student has a different pattern of these characteristics.

Although there is some unavoidable overlap, we have organized the characteristics of learning disabled college students into seven categories: cognitive, language, perceptual-motor, academic, work and study habits, social, and affective. This grouping is very similar to the specific domains used by Cronin and Gerber (1982) when summarizing the characteristics of learning disabled adolescents.*

COGNITIVE

It is difficult to make a generalization about the level of overall cognitive ability of learning disabled college students. IQ levels of these students vary as a function of each program's view of the IQ level needed for success. When it was felt that learning disabled students needed above average intelligence to be successful in college, reported IQs were in the high average range. When IQ was not deemed to be as important for success in college, reported mean IQs were lower. The only possible generalization was that when IQ scores were reported for students in learning disabilities college programs, they were no lower than an IQ of 85.

Some specific accounts of learning disabled college students' functioning on the Wechsler Adult Intelligence Scale (WAIS) were available (Cordoni, 1979a; Cordoni, O'Donnell, Ramanach, Kurtz, and Rosenshein, 1981; Saddler, personal communication, July 14, 1982). These reports indicated Verbal IQ to be higher than Performance IQ, with higher scores on Bannatyne's (1974) spatial factor (comprised of the Picture Completion, Block Design, and Object Assembly subtests) and Verbal Conceptualization factor (Comprehension, Similarities, and Vocabulary subtests), than on the sequential factor (Digit Span, Arithmetic, and Coding subtests) and acquired knowledge factor (Information, Arithmetic, and Vocabulary subtests). Performance on the Digit Span subtest was particularly low. (A description of the subtests of the WAIS appears in Chapter 6 of this handbook).

---

*Our sources of information included: Barbaro, 1982; Blalock and Dixon, 1982; Brown, 1982; Chesler, 1980; Cordoni, 1979a, 1980, 1982a, 1982b; Rosenthal, Fine, and deVight, 1982; Vogel, 1982; Vogel and Adelman, 1981; Vogel and Moran, 1982; Vogel and Sattler, 1981; Webb, 1974; Worcester, 1981; Worden, Malmgren, and Gabourie, 1982; Worden and Nakamura, 1982; personal communications from: J. Barsch, July, 1982; B. Cordoni, June 21, 1982; I. Götz, September, 1982; J. McGuire, October, 1982; R. Nash, June 17, 1982; P. Quinlan, July 16, 1982; and D. Saddler, July 14, 1982.

Learning disabled college students typically have difficulty with the following.

Acquiring a fund of information about the world
Sequencing events and ideas
Understanding abstract concepts
Spontaneously employing cognitive strategies
Switching strategies as appropriate
Distinguishing important from unimportant information
Reasoning in a deductive manner
Perceiving cause-and-effect relationships
Remembering things seen and heard (short- and longterm)
Sustaining attention to tasks
Organizing ideas and information
Generalizing skills from one task and situation to another

LANGUAGE

Language difficulties are the core of learning disabilities. The definition of specific learning disabilities appearing in Public Law 94-142, the Education for All Handicapped Children Act, states that a specific learning disability refers to a disorder in one or more of the basic psychological processes involved in understanding or in using spoken or written language. Deficits in both spoken and written language are characteristic of college learning disabled students. These deficits interfere with performance in virtually all courses taken by these students. Learning disabled college students typically have difficulty with the following.

Spoken Language
Grasping what others say to them
Using mature syntactical patterns
Using an appropriate range of vocabulary
Retrieving the appropriate word for a situation
Using words in their appropriate context

Written Language
Expressing themselves precisely and clearly
Using a variety of sentence structures
Using mature syntactical patterns
Using an appropriate range of words

Using long and/or difficult words
Organizing thoughts
Using punctuation correctly
Using a sufficient number of verbs, adjectives, and adverbs
Writing compositions of sufficient length for the purpose

PERCEPTUAL-MOTOR

Perceptual-motor deficits are one of the primary characteristics of young learning disabled children. It is generally believed that these deficits phase out as the learning disabled child matures. We found, however, that professionals working with college learning disabled students reported that perceptual-motor problems were still present among some of these students. Learning disabled college students sometimes have difficulty with the following.

Perceiving the correct orientation of complex visual figures
Perceiving spatial attributes
Dealing with three-dimensional figures and arrays
Discriminating complex visual designs and configurations
Forming a visual Gestalt
Locating specific information on a page
Discriminating complex sounding words
Performing tasks requiring fine motor coordination

ACADEMIC

We were consistently told that learning disabled college students had deficits in all basic skills areas. Individual students typically had deficits in one or all of the basic skills of reading, spelling, handwriting, and mathematics. Reported achievement levels for basic skills ranged from third grade to college level. Learning disabled college students typically have difficulty with the following. .

Reading
   Applying phonics rules and generalizations
   Decoding unfamiliar words
   Understanding what was read
   Determining main ideas
   Maintaining an efficient rate of reading
   Adapting reading rate to specific reading purposes

Spelling

    Maintaining the correct sequence of letters when spelling words
    Perceiving sound–letter correspondence when spelling words
    Spelling irregular words
    Spelling complex words

Handwriting

    Establishing a comfortable style of writing
    Maintaining an efficient rate of writing
    Writing in cursive
    Forming legible letters
    Forming letters of appropriate size
    Forming letters of consistent size throughout the same paper
    Producing neat papers
    Keeping writing within the margins
    Gripping the pencil properly
    Using upper case letters correctly
    Maintaining writing quality when time limits are involved such as during
        timed tests or taking notes from lectures

Mathematics

    Doing computations
    Mastering the multiplication tables
    Reasoning mathematically
    Solving mathematical problems
    Recalling the sequence of an operational process
    Understanding and retaining terms representing quantitative concepts

WORK AND STUDY HABITS

As learning disabled students progress through school, efficient and effective work and study habits become increasingly important. By the college level, these work and study habits are of crucial significance. Learning disabled college students were described as generally lacking good work and study habits. Learning disabled college students typically have difficulty with the following.

Organizing and budgeting time
Completing work when due
Getting work started
Sustaining effort on a task
Establishing short- and longterm goals and objectives
Identifying the essential requirements of a task
Integrating information from various sources
Using library resources
Using the dictionary and other reference tools
Taking complete and accurate notes
Outlining important information in a text
Controlling test anxiety

SOCIAL

Increasing attention is being given to the social difficulties experienced by learning disabled children. The social difficulties experienced by these children apparently carry over into young adulthood. Cordoni (1982b) has identified social functioning as a major problem area for learning disabled college students. Her view is supported by many other professionals who are working with this population. Learning disabled college students typically have difficulty with the following.

Establishing good relationships with others
Making friends
Working effectively with others
Maintaining appropriate family relationships
Reading body language and facial expressions
Manifesting appropriate social behaviors
Saying what is thought or felt
Avoiding saying or doing things that are later regretted
Knowing what to say in a situation
Understanding humor and sarcasm
Engaging in "small talk"
Developing and maintaining hobbies and interests
Maintaining appropriate personal appearance
Relating to authority figures such as professors and advisors

AFFECTIVE

A wide range of affective characteristics was reported in descriptions of learning disabled college students. These affective characteristics represent emotional or feeling states. They occurred in varying patterns and degrees for any given student. Learning disabled college students typically have difficulty with the following.

Establishing a positive self-concept
Establishing a sense of security
Establishing a sense of competence
Developing self-confidence
Avoiding overdependence on others
Accepting criticism by others
Adjusting to the feelings of others
Tolerating frustration
Viewing their life prospects optimistically
Trusting others
Acting maturely
Clarifying their values about life
Meeting responsibilities
Curbing impulsive behavior
Subordinating their own welfare to that of others
Maintaining motivation
Controlling anxiety
Interacting with others in a nondefensive manner

It is important to respond to these characteristics when planning and developing programs for learning disabled college students. The following checklist (Table 3-1) may be duplicated and used when programming students. The appropriate characteristics for a student can be checked as information is obtained from reports of previous work with the student by High School teachers and learning disability specialists, diagnostic testing (see Chapter 6 of this handbook), and observations of and interviews with the student once he or she enters the program. Program services can then be developed to remediate and/or compensate for these characteristics.

Table 3-1 Checklist of Characteristics of Learning Disabled College Students

Name of student _____

Date of entry in program _____

Name of advisor _____

Instructions: Based upon your review of previous records and current data, check each characteristic that applies to this student. Check only those that are clearly evident. Use these characteristics to develop programming recommendations. Write these recommendations in the last section of this form.

Cognitive

_____ Poor fund of information about the world

_____ Difficulty sequencing events and ideas

_____ Difficulty understanding abstract concepts

_____ Poor ability to spontaneously employ cognitive strategies

_____ Poor ability to switch strategies as appropriate

_____ Poor ability to distinguish important from unimportant information

_____ Difficulty reasoning in a deductive manner

_____ Little awareness of cause-and-effect relationships

_____ Poor long- and shortterm auditory and visual memory

_____ Difficulty sustaining attention to tasks

_____ Poor ability to organize ideas and information

_____ Poor ability to generalize skills from one task and situation to another

Language

Spoken Language

_____ Difficulty grasping what others say to them

_____ Immature syntactical patterns

_____ Limited range of vocabulary

    Difficulty retrieving the appropriate word for a situation

    Inappropriate use of words

Written Language

    Imprecise and unclear expression

    Repeated use of a small variety of sentence structures

    Immature syntactical patterns

    Use of a restricted set of words

    Infrequent use of long words

    Poor organization of thoughts

    Incorrect use of punctuation

    Infrequent use of long or difficult words

    Underutilization of verbs, adjectives, and adverbs

    Compositions usually too short for purpose

Perceptual-Motor

    Reversals, rotations and inversions of letters and numerals

    Difficulty perceiving spatial attributes

    Difficulty dealing with three dimensional figures and arrays

    Difficulty discriminating complex visual designs and configurations

    Difficulty forming a visual Gestalt

    Difficulty locating specific information on a page

    Difficulty discriminating complex sounding words

    Imprecise fine motor coordination

Academic

   Reading

    Gaps in knowledge of phonics

    Poor word attack skills

(continued)

Table 3-1 (continued)

_____ Poor ability to understand what was read
_____ Poor ability to determine main ideas
_____ Slow rate of reading
_____ Failure to adapt reading rate to specific reading purposes

Spelling

_____ Transposition of letters when spelling words
_____ Omission or substitution of sounds when spelling words
_____ Attempts to phonetically spell irregular words
_____ General avoidance of writing words that are difficult to spell

Handwriting

_____ Awkward and uncomfortable style of writing
_____ Slow rate of writing
_____ Tendency to use manuscript rather than cursive
_____ Poorly formed or illegible letters
_____ Writing that is overly large
_____ Writing that varies in size throughout the same paper
_____ Papers that are generally sloppy
_____ Difficulty keeping writing within the margins
_____ Improper pencil grip
_____ Overuse of upper case letters
_____ Deterioration of writing quality when time limits are involved such as during timed
       tests or taking notes from lectures

Mathematics

_____ Poor computational skills
_____ Incomplete memorization of multiplication tables
_____ Poor mathematical reasoning
_____ Poor ability to solve mathematical problems

_____ Difficulty recalling the sequence of an operational process
_____ Failure to understand and retain terms representing quantitative concepts

Work and Study Habits

_____ Poor organization and budgeting of time
_____ Difficulty completing work when due
_____ Difficulty getting work started
_____ Difficulty sustaining effort on a task
_____ Difficulty establishing short- and longterm goals and objectives
_____ Inability to identify the essential requirements of a task
_____ Difficulty integrating information from various sources
_____ Unfamiliarity with library resources
_____ Difficulty using the dictionary and other reference tools
_____ Notes that are typically sparse, incomplete and inaccurate
_____ Difficulty outlining important information in a text
_____ Excessive test anxiety

Social

_____ Difficulty establishing good relationships with others
_____ Difficulty making friends
_____ Difficulty working effectively with others
_____ Poor family relationships
_____ Difficulty reading body language and facial expressions
_____ Inappropriate social behaviors
_____ Problems saying what is thought or felt
_____ Regretting what was said or done
_____ Uncertainty of knowing what to say in a situation
_____ Misunderstanding humor and sarcasm

(continued)

Table 3-1 (continued)

_____ Difficulty engaging in "small talk"
_____ Few hobbies and interests
_____ Insufficient attention to personal appearance
_____ Difficulty relating to authority figures such as professors and advisors

Affective

_____ Low sense of self-esteem
_____ Feelings of insecurity
_____ Feelings of inferiority
_____ Lack of self-confidence
_____ Overdependence on others
_____ Vulnerability to criticism by others
_____ Hypersensitivity to the feelings of others
_____ Low tolerance for frustration
_____ Generally pessimistic about outcomes of own efforts
_____ Suspicious of the motives of others
_____ General immaturity
_____ Unclarified values about life
_____ Unable to meet responsibilities
_____ Tendency to respond impulsively
_____ Overconcern with own welfare
_____ Low degree of motivation
_____ Excessive anxiety about things
_____ Defensiveness in interacting with others

Recommendations

(a) *Tutoring*

(b) *Remediation*

(c) *Instructional strategies*

(d) *Special courses*

(e) *Academic program advisement*

(f) *Counseling*

(g) *Other*

Name of recorder _____

Position _____

Date _____

4

Developing a Learning
Disabilities Program

More college programs for students with learning disabilities are needed. The few comprehensive programs available cannot service the substantial number of learning disabled students now seeking to attend college. To adequately service this population, the programs must be comprehensive in nature and deal with the varying characteristics associated with learning disabilities in college students that were discussed in the preceding chapter.

Our initial examination of college programs that claim to provide services for the learning disabled revealed that most of the programs provided no services beyond those which they already provided for the non–learning-disabled population. Experience seems to demonstrate that such programs fall far short of the needs of the learning disabled students. Directors of learning disability programs reported that when comprehensive services were not available for learning disabled college students, the students frequently did not make it beyond the first year of college. On the other hand, where comprehensive programs were available the retention rate was very high.

Those colleges and universities interested in serving learning disabled students should do so by establishing comprehensive programs. A comprehensive program is one that provides such services as differentiated testing for admission, remediation of basic skills, assistance in learning course content, and counseling. It is staffed by an interdisciplinary group of professionals including learning disability specialists, reading specialists, psychologists, and counselors, and has the active support of subject area professors.

This chapter will explain how successful college programs for learning disabled students were developed at a number of colleges and universities.

Through an examination of exemplary programs, we discovered that, in most cases, a common set of steps were followed for developing these programs. We advise those who are interested in developing new programs to consider following these steps.

IDENTIFYING THE CATALYST

Every successful program needs someone to champion its cause. The same is true for college programs for learning disabled students, most of which programs come about through the efforts of one individual committed to providing higher education opportunities for learning disabled students. It is upon this person's shoulders that the responsibility falls for initiating the steps to bring learning disability programs to fruition at an institution.

Typically, this individual needs to be a professor of considerable reputation with much teaching experience and political sense. The person's reputation will give credence to the arguments he or she makes for higher education opportunities for learning disabled students. The teaching experience will enable this catalyst to convince subject area professors to alter their teaching and testing styles. The political experience will enable the catalyst to obtain the administrative support for a college program for learning disabled students and to obtain approval for the program from a myriad of college or university committees.

Knowledge of learning disabilities is probably the most important competency needed by the catalyst. The catalyst must fully understand the characteristics of learning disabled college students in order to provide them with programs that are flexible, comprehensive, and interdisciplinary. Such persons are usually found in learning disability teacher training programs within the concerned college or university and they usually have extensive experience working with learning disabled adolescents and adults.

CONVINCING THE ADMINISTRATION

Any program, to be successful, must be supported by the administration of a college or university. There are three possible ways to convince administrators to provide higher education opportunities for qualified learning disabled students. It may take elements of all three to convince some administrators to enter the new program area and provide educational opportunities for learning disabled students.

One common approach used for convincing administrators is to argue that providing higher education opportunities for qualified learning disabled students is part of the social mission of any college or university. Most administrators have no difficulty understanding the need to provide higher education oportunities for visual or hearing handicapped students. Administrators may not be quite as receptive to the idea of providing similar educational opportunities for the learning disabled. Because of their lack of understanding of learning disabilities, many college and university administrators unfortunately still think of the learning disabled as lazy or lacking the intelligence to do college work.

Given the decline in college and university enrollments throughout the country, many college administrators have become more ready to service learning disabled students. Learning disabled students provide a new source of tuition revenue that has largely been untapped in this country. Our survey suggests that parents of learning disabled students are willing to pay fees in addition to tuition costs in order to obtain college educations for their children.

The third and most convincing argument is for compliance with Section 504 of the Rehabilitation Act of 1973, which was signed into law in 1977. This law should be reviewed by anyone interested in convincing college and university administrators of the need to service qualified learning disabled students. Chapter 2 contains an extensive presentation of Section 504.

Reducing Administrators' Concerns

Naturally, administrators are fearful of any program that might alter the image of their college or university. Administrators need to be convinced that by servicing qualified learning disabled students their university will not become known as a college for learning disabled students. We found this to be a greater concern for administrators in small colleges than for those in large universities. Among the program directors of learning disabilities college programs we interviewed, there was a consensus that there was no change in a college's image as long as the population of learning disabled students did not exceed 10 percent of the base population.

Cost effectiveness is also one of the common concerns expressed by college administrators. Learning disabilities college programs are expensive to operate due to the high cost of providing comprehensive services. Parents of learning disabled students, however, seem to be more than willing to pay an additional fee for the comprehensive services their children need to make it through college. Program directors reported that the special fees charged by their institutions ranged from a few hundred to several thousand dollars per year.

IDENTIFYING THE DIRECTOR

The person who served as the initial catalyst for the learning disabilities college program frequently became the first program director. Whereas the catalyst worked informally, the director works formally as the driving force behind all aspects of program development.

The director should have technical knowledge of learning disabilities, good interpersonal skills and administrative experience. Knowledge of learning disabilities is necessary to establish a comprehensive learning disabilities program. Interpersonal skills are needed for working with faculty members and administrators to help them understand the nature of learning disabilities and the types of services these students need to succeed in college. Administrative experience is needed to hire and supervise staff and to prepare and monitor the budget and logistics of the program.

We asked a number of directors of college programs for learning disabled students how important the selection of a director was to the overall success of a program. They assured us that this decision was probably the single most important decision having bearing upon the success of a program.

CONVINCING THE FACULTY

One of the first responsibilities of the program director will be to work with the faculty to convince them of the need to provide services to learning disabled college students. Program directors told us that they spent hundreds of hours winning the support of their faculty members. This activity typically begins long before the first learning disabled student arrives on campus and continues throughout the program's existence.

Working with faculty is probably the most challenging job a learning disabilities program director will have. In a communication with the authors on June 29, 1982, Martin reported that she had not obtained the full support of her faculty before she began her learning disabled college program. She consequently had to spend considerable time backpedaling to develop the necessary faculty support for a successful program. In a similar communication (July, 1982), Barsch indicated that personal contact was the key to winning faculty support. He went to department meetings to explain the learning disabilities program and its services, and met with individual faculty members to further solicit their support and to answer any of their questions. The program directors we interviewed recommended unanimously that faculty awareness programs have the director's personal touch. Personal contact worked much better than memos, forms, and large group meetings. Vogel (communication, June 16, 1982) recommended providing orientation sessions for new faculty members as well as renewal workshops for continuing faculty members at the beginning of each term.

Cordoni reported on June 21, 1982, that she prepared a slide/tape presentation that she used to promote her program at faculty meetings. Her slide/tape presentation answered thrèe basic questions: What are learning disabilities? What can be done about learning disabilities? and, How do learning disabled students fit into a university setting? Cordoni's slide/tape presentation has been used by a number of learning disabilities program directors to answer these same questions for faculties on their campuses.

Cordoni also distributed articles to interested faculty members. The articles explained what learning disabled students were like and what they needed to succeed in college. Some directors suggested that faculty members be introduced to small groups of learning disabled students so they could learn about learning disabilities directly from the students. A director has to be creative to find ways to break through professors' preoccupations and convince them that qualified learning disabled students deserve a chance to succeed in their classes.

Many college professors are concerned that by having learning disabled students in their classes the class standards will be lowered. College professors need to be reassured that learning disabled students must be required to meet the same standards as all other students. The degrees earned by learning disabled students must be equivalent to the degrees earned by the other students studying the same curriculum.

Faculty members are also concerned about the additional time they will be required to spend working with learning disabled students. Faculty members are, naturally, protective of the time they need for class preparation, research, and community and college service. Faculty members must be assured that they will need to do only a few things differently when learning disabled students are in their classes. They must know that the bulk of the work for preparing learning disabled students for colleges will fall upon the learning disability program and its staff.

It is important for the director to identify the influential faculty members and single them out for special intensive contact. An influential faculty member may provide access to an entire area, department, or even a college. The directors we interviewed were all aware of the influential faculty members at their colleges and worked through these influentials to reach other faculty members.

Probably one of the most difficult things for the directors of the learning disabilities program to overcome will be existing myths about learning disabilities in the minds of faculty members. Directors can expect to find faculty members who have a limited perception of learning disabilities and see it as another name for mental retardation. Or they may find faculty members who believe that learning disabilities are caused by emotional problems or that the learning disabled have insufficient intelligence to succeed in college. Learning disabled students themselves are a valuable resource for countering these myths. Successful learning disabilities students who perform well in courses will convince faculty members of the worthiness of the learning disabilities program. For this reason, Vogel recommended on June 16, 1982, beginning the college learning disabilities program with a small, carefully selected group of students whose probability for success is quite high.

FORMING A PLANNING TEAM

To continue the process of developing a learning disabilities college program, the director should form a planning team. A planning team approach to program development provides a broad basis for support of the program as well as assuring that the program is appropriate for the institution. Under the director's leadership, the planning team should work to meet three major objectives: to learn about the nature of learning disabled college students; to acquire an understanding of the services needed by learning disabled students to succeed in college; and to formulate the generalizations upon which the learning disabled college program should be developed.

Learning disabled students need a broad range of services in order to be successful in college. To provide these services, the planning team should have representatives from many different units of the college or university. The directors we interviewed began looking for planning team members among the teaching faculty in schools of education, English, math, and science departments. Vogel further recommended that the search be extended to the Office of the Dean of Students, Office of Handicapped Students Services, Guidance and Counseling Departments, Evaluation Center, Health Services, Library, and the Media Center. Members from other appropriate units as the director so decides should also be included on the planning team.

When the planning team members have been identified, it is necessary for the director to begin a series of activities to help them achieve their major objectives. Most program directors recommended the following. Circulate materials to planning team members to help them understand the characteristics of learning disabled students. Also, circulate descriptions of successful learning disabled programs at other colleges. Have some planning team members attend professional conferences to learn more about the characteristics and needs of learning disabled students. Have other planning team members visit ongoing learning disabled college programs. Planning team members should plan on spending two or three days on the campus they visit. They should request opportunities to speak with the program director, college administrators, admissions officers, housing director, faculty members and staff of the learning disabled program. They should also be sure to request an opportunity to speak to representative learning disabled college students.

Once the team members understand the characteristics and needs of the learning disabled college student, they are ready to plan the learning disability program for their own college or university. This needs to be done under the careful leadership of the program director. The planning team should continue to serve as an entity until the program is implemented. Some directors told us that they believed it was important for the planning team to continue to serve as an advisory board throughout the existence of the learning disabled college program.

STAFFING THE PROGRAM

Any program with 25 or more students will need a fulltime director, assistant director, psychoeducational diagnostician, a number of basic skills remediation specialists, subject area tutors, and adjuncts. Programs with fewer than 25 students will probably not be able to justify the number and variety of staff members required to run a comprehensive program for learning disabled college students. It is important to note that people are the major resource of any learning disability college program. While some equipment and materials are necessary, the success of programs largely rests on securing well trained and enthusiastic staff members.

Director

The director has many responsibilities. To meet these responsibilities, the director will usually be involved in the following activities.

1. Serve as an advocate for the learning disabilities program
2. Meet with administrators to discuss the operation and size of the learning disability program
3. Meet with faculty members to inform them of the services provided to learning disabled students through the program
4. Hire staff members
5. Manage the overall operation of the program
6. Meet with groups of learning disabled high school students and their

teachers to explain the learning disability program

7. Participate in admissions decisions
8. Supervise staff members
9. Develop and teach selected courses on special techniques for working with learning disabled students
10. Provide counseling and advisement to students
11. Serve as a liaison with parents

Assistant Director

Most programs will need an assistant director to work along with the program director. The assistant director must be someone who supports the philosophic position of the director and who is an equally strong advocate for the program. The assistant director's primary responsibility would be to qualify new students for the program. To meet this and other responsibilities, the assistant director will need to perform many of the following activities.

1. Answer telephone and letter inquiries regarding the program
2. Assemble high school records for all applicants
3. Request copies of psychoeducational evaluations on all applicants
4. Schedule prospective students for a visit to the campus
5. Arrange for individual testing for those students for whom reports on psychoeducational evaluations are not available
6. Prepare reports with recommendations on admissions for the learning disability program admissions committee
7. Schedule students for college classes
8. Schedule students for subject area tutoring and basic skills instruction
9. Make arrangements to have textbooks audio recorded
10. Participate in admissions conferences
11. Speak to groups of learning disabled high school students and their teachers about the services available through the learning disability program
12. Teach selected courses on special techniques for working with learning disabled students
13. Provide counseling and advisement to students
14. Serve as a liaison with parents

Psychoeducational Diagnostician

At least one psychoeducational diagnostician will be needed to complete the diagnostic testing to identify the specific educational needs of the learning disabled students. Sometimes this role is assumed and shared by the director and assistant director. In larger programs, the continued need for evaluations will require a fulltime person to fill this role. To accomplish this role, the psychoeducational diagnostician will be involved in the activities that follow.

1. Gather and interpret information on program applicants such as: school records; social, emotional and language development; nature of the learning disability; physical disabilities beyond the learning disability; and prior psychoeducational evaluations.
2. Administer psychoeducational tests such as: intelligence, achievement, and personality tests; and tests appropriate for evaluating aspects of the learning disability.
3. Develop an Individual Educational Plan (IEP) describing goals and objectives related to: tutoring, remediation, counseling, special courses, and techniques for working with the student.

Basic Skills Remediation Specialists

Specially trained learning disability teachers are necessary to provide the basic skills remediation students need to handle their subject area responsibilities. Basic skills remediation specialists provide instruction in one or more of the following areas: reading, writing, spelling, mathematics, expressive oral language, listening, use of compensatory strategies, and use of study skills.

Subject Area Tutors

Many learning disabled students will need subjects area tutors to help them understand the content they will be exposed to in college level courses. These tutors are needed to help the learning disabled student bridge the gap between the information learned in high school and what is required in college. Frequently, learning disabled students are not exposed to as much subject area information as are non–learning-disabled students in high school. This knowledge void must be made up by tutors. The tutors are also necessary to help the learning disabled students learn how to study in the various subject areas. The most common areas in which tutors are necessary are English, mathematics, physical science, social sciences, and foreign language.

In the learning disability programs we visited, we found that tutors came from three major sources. The program philosophy and program fees usually dictated which source of tutors was used. The sources of tutors included the following.

1. *Non–learning-disabled students.* Typically, these were junior and senior students who were majoring in the area in which they served

as tutors. They generally had received either an A or B grade in the course in which they were serving as a tutor.

2. *Outside professionals.*   Typically, these were high school teachers or spouses of faculty members who were very knowledgeable in the subject area in which they served as tutors.

3. *College faculty members.*   In some cases, college faculty members held special tutoring sessions for students having difficulty in their classes. The faculty members provided tutoring only for courses they taught.

Adjuncts

Because of the many special services offered to learning disabled students, it is necessary to have adjunct personnel available. These personnel perform such tasks as the following.

1. Proctoring the administration of tests administered to learning disabled students under untimed or other special conditions
2. Attending classes and serving as notetakers for learning disabled students
3. Preparing audio tapes of study materials
4. Serving as taped-text librarians

The personnel needed to operate a college learning disabled program varied with the philosophy and type of services that constituted the program. Most programs were staffed minimally with the six different classes of personnel identified here.

HOUSING THE PROGRAM

Our examination of programs for learning disabled students revealed that the programs were typically housed in one of three areas within the college or university. Where a program was housed seemed to have more to do with where the impetus for the program came from rather than any other factor. The location of the program appeared to be unrelated to the program's effectiveness.

Special Education Department

By housing the learning disability program in a Special Education Department, it can be beneficial to both the learning disabled students as well as students in the special education teacher training program. Undergraduate students can gain valuable experience by providing tutoring and remediation to the learning disabled students. Graduate students can supervise the undergraduate students as well as work directly with the learning disabled students. Housing the program in the Special Education Department is most appropriate when there is an existing professional staff and teacher-training program in learning disabilities.

Office of Handicapped Student Services

This may also be an appropriate place to house a learning disabled program. This would be particularly so if within the Office of Handicapped Student Services there are professionals who are particularly knowledge-able about learning disabilities. We found a few cases where the most supportive atmosphere for the development of a learning disability college program was within the Office of Handicapped Student Services.

Office of the Dean of Students

If the college does not have a Department of Special Education and if the Office of Handicapped Student Services cannot house a learning disability program then the program could be housed in the Office of the Dean of Students. Of course, to do this, it would be necessary for someone in that office to have considerable knowledge of learning disabilities and have sufficient time to foster the development of the program.

FUNDING THE PROGRAM

Our examination of learning disability programs revealed that they were funded from a variety of sources. Usually, only in state institutions were the programs fully supported by their sponsoring institution. In these state institutions, no fees were charged to the students beyond the usual tuition and activity fees.

At private institutions, there usually was a special fee charged for the program's services. Some institutions charged a flat fee for each semester the learning disabled student was in the program. In other cases, the fees were graduated with higher fees charged for the first year and reduced fees for subsequent years. Those institutions that followed this graduated policy believed that as services to students were reduced, the fees should be correspondingly reduced.

Program directors we interviewed at private colleges and universities told us that the fees charged by their institutions at most covered the expenses of the learning disabled program. Obviously, learning disabled programs do not produce additional monies for the general fund of the institution offering such programs. The only funds to be gained are from the additional tuition dollars brought about by additional enrollments in the institution.

A few programs have received federal funding through the Regional Postsecondary Education Program for Deaf and Other Handicapped Persons. Funds from this source may be used for providing services needed by handicapped students to succeed in college. The funds may not be used for payment of tuition or subsistence allowance, nor for cost of construction. Appendix 4 contains information about Federal programs that provide funding possibilities for postsecondary educational institutions providing services to disabled students.

5

Admitting Learning Disabled
Students to College

Prior to the issuing of the 1977 regulations implementing Subpart E of Section 504 of the Rehabilitation Act of 1973, learning disabled students found it difficult to be admitted to four-year colleges. The impact of Subpart E of Section 504 upon admissions procedures was revealed in Chapter 2. Basically, this law forbids colleges from using different standards for admitting learning disabled applicants than they do for non–learning-disabled applicants. The law also forbids the use for admissions decisions of test results that reflect the disabilities of learning disabled applicants rather than their potential for doing college work.

TYPES OF ADMISSION POLICIES

There are three types of admission policies commonly used in colleges and universities throughout the United States. Admission policies determine who is admitted to a college or university. Any college may have more than one admission policy in effect.

Open Admission

This policy requires an applicant to have only a high school diploma or its equivalent to be granted admission to a college. Typically, open admission policies are found at junior or community colleges. Learning disabled students with high school diplomas or their equivalents have no difficulty gaining entrance to colleges with an open admission policy.

Regular Admission

This policy requires an applicant to have a high school diploma or its equivalent and provide grade point average (GPA), rank in graduating class, and scores on standardized tests such as the Scholastic Aptitude Test (SAT) or the American College Testing Program (ACT). This policy is most commonly found in effect at four-year colleges and universities. It is the policy by which most students are admitted to these colleges and universities. Learning disabled students find it difficult to gain admission to colleges and universities when only a regular admission policy is in effect.

Special Admission

This policy allows each student to be considered for admission to a college or university on a case-by-case approach. Under this policy, flexible entrance criteria are used and varied sources and types of information are sought out. Many schools with regular admissions policies also have special admissions policies to maintain flexibility in student selection.

Subpart E of Section 504 has had considerable impact upon all three admissions policies. Those institutions using open admissions policies must admit learning disabled students with high school diplomas or their equivalent with the same ease as other applicants. Institutions requiring GPA, rank in graduating class, and SAT or ACT test results must carefully examine their admissions policy to be sure that the information they are gathering does not reflect the learning disability of a student rather than the student's potential for college. A special admissions policy enables an institution to circumvent the problems of regular admission related to compliance with Subpart E of Section 504.

Special admission is clearly the predominant procedure used to admit students to learning disability college programs. Colleges offering special admission to learning disabled students require that they be admitted to the college's learning disabilities program at the same time they are admitted to the college. We refer to this as a cooperative admissions process.

COOPERATIVE ADMISSION PROCESS

Colleges with learning disabilities programs typically require that the learning disabled applicant make simultaneous application to the program and the college. Usually, two different admissions forms and procedures are used. The admission decision for the learning disabilities program is typically made by the program director or by the program admission committee. Eventually, the admission decision for the college is made by the Director of Admission or the College Admission Committee.

The learning disability program director or a designated person or committee is responsible for evaluating each applicant. After the evaluation, the program director forwards a recommendation to the college Director of Admission. Because both the program director and the Director of Admission are looking for intelligent, knowledgeable, and emotionally and socially mature students who could succeed in college, the recommendations from the program director are usually supported by the college's Director of Admission.

Here are the typical steps a learning disabled applicant goes through to gain admission to a college through the cooperative admission process.

The applicant sends letters of inquiry to the Director of College Admission and the Director of the learning disabilities program. In the letters, the applicant requests a college bulletin, application forms for the college, and application forms and descriptive materials for the learning disabilities program.

The applicant carefully completes the application forms for the college and the learning disabilities program. Program directors told us they preferred to have the applicants complete the forms in their own handwriting. Since the application form is the applicant's first contact with the college and the learning disability program, it is important that the form be completed as specified, is legible, and provides the best possible image of the applicant. All forms should be submitted to the appropriate office with the checks covering the typical nonrefundable fees charged for application.

Usually, the applicant is required to submit evidence of a learning disability. The evidence may be as simple as a letter from the applicant's high school learning disability teacher specifying the nature of the learning disability and the period of time the applicant has been enrolled in a learning disabilities program. Some institutions require substantially more evidence, which may include a report from a qualified psychoeducational diagnostician specifying the nature of the disability and including test scores. Most program directors request that test scores from the Wechsler Adult Intelligence Scale (WAIS) or its later edition, the Wechsler Adult Intelligence Scale—Revised (WAIS—R), be included as part of the psycho-educational report.

The applicant submits transcripts showing the total number of credits earned while in high school, rank in graduating class, and GPA. It is advisable to have the high school transcript record show that the applicant is learning disabled, and the number of years enrolled in a learning disability program. This provides further evidence of the nature of the handicap. An applicant who has attended other colleges must also submit transcripts from each college attended.

Many colleges request that the learning disabled applicant also submit scores from standardized college entrance examinations such as the SAT or ACT. The applicants are generally advised to take an alternative version of these college entrance examinations.

The SAT has two subtests: Verbal and Mathematics. The Verbal subtest measures vocabulary knowledge and reading comprehension. The Mathematics subtest measures quantitative abilities closely related to college work. The SAT is available in four special editions (regular-size type, large type, Braille, and audio cassette). Learning disabled students may take the most appropriate edition with extended time limits. They may also use a reader as necessary. For a sample test booklet and additional information write: ATP: Services for Handicapped Students, Institutional Services, Box 2891, Princeton, NJ 08541; or, call: (609) 921-9000 (Ask for Institutional Services).

The ACT has four academic subtests: English, mathematics, social studies, and natural sciences. This test provides information on educational development and ability to do college work. Learning disabled students may use a reader, a regular test form, audio cassettes, and/or arrangements for individual testing conditions with longer time limits. For a sample test booklet and additional information, write: ACT Test Administration, P.O. Box 168, Iowa City, IA 52243; or, call: (319) 337-1332.

Not all colleges having learning disability programs require their applicants to take standardized college entrance examinations. Those requiring an entrance examination use the results to estimate the level of knowledge a student has acquired. Typically, no cutoff score is used.

An applicant is often required to submit a handwritten essay describing some aspect of the applicant's life or elaborating on specified questions. The handwritten essay is evaluated for cognitive clarity and legibility.

Once all the application forms, transcripts and other records, letters, test scores, reports, and the handwritten essay are received, they are reviewed by the learning disability program staff. In some cases, this is done by an admission committee formed from staff members of the learning disabilities program. In other cases, it may be the director and assistant director, or the director alone. The applicant's file is reviewed to answer the following questions.

Does the applicant have a learning disability? Most program directors we spoke to required applicants to provide clear evidence of their learning disability. They frequently look for evidence that the applicant had been diagnosed as learning disabled by a qualified psychoeducational diagnostician who used a wide range of instruments. Transcripts were examined for evidence that the applicant had been placed in a learning disability program. Letters from the applicant's learning disabilities high school teachers were read to further verify that the applicant was learning disabled. At Adelphi University, each applicant had to submit a copy of an individual educational plan (IEP) that had been used to provide services while the applicant was in high school (Barbaro, 1982). Letters or reports from psychologists, physicians, and school counselors were also examined to verify that the applicant was learning disabled.

Does the applicant have the intellectual ability to do college work? As Webb pointed out in a communication on July 15, 1982, colleges must be able to differentiate between those applicants with the ability to do college work and those applicants whose parents hope college will transform them into scholars. To do this, the staff of the learning disabilty program uses the results of individually administered intelligence tests such as the Wechsler Adult Intelligence Scale (WAIS), Wechsler Adult Intelligence Scale—Revised (WAIS–R), Slosson Intelligence Test, and the Ravens Standard Progressive Matrices.

Most program directors reported that they preferred to make decisions on intellectual ability using the results from the WAIS or WAIS–R rather than other intelligence tests. Webb looked for college level thinking ability as evidenced by Scaled scores of 13 or higher on the Comprehension, Similarities, and Block Design subtests of the WAIS/WAIS–R. Cordoni et al. (1981) suggested that the ACID cluster (Arithmetic, Comprehension, Information, and Digit Span subtests) on the WAIS/WAIS–R could be useful for making decisions about college potential. Among program directors, there are some who believe that learning disabled students with IQs as low as 90 could succeed in college if they had sufficient motivation to do so.

From our discussions with program directors, it is clear that learning disabled students with a wide range of abilities are being admitted to college. It is also clear that learning disability programs are designed for students with at least average intellectual ability. The variations in IQ levels accepted for admission to various colleges with learning disability programs appear to be related to the intellectual study of the student body at a specific college.

What knowledge has the applicant acquired? To form an opinion about a non–learning-disabled applicant's level of knowledge, admissions personnel examine GPA, rank in graduating class, and SAT or ACT scores. Saddler (communication, July 14, 1982) questions the usefulness of using GPA for making admissions decisions about learning disabled applicants. Saddler believes that GPA for learning disabled applicants is largely a function of the quality of the special education services provided by high schools. We suspect that rank in graduating class may have little relevance by the same logic. Scores on standard administrations of the SAT or ACT do little more than reflect the learning disability of the applicant.

There are three things done through special admission to provide a more valid estimate of a learning disabled applicant's general knowledge.

1. Examine the results from the alternative administration of the SAT or ACT. The subtest scores may reveal areas where the applicant lacks knowledge.
2. Request letters from English, math, science, and other high school subject area teachers describing the applicant's knowledge in these subject areas. Vernoy, on June 17, 1982, recommended this procedure for gaining insights into acquired knowledge.
3. Require the applicant to visit the campus and be interviewed by personnel from the learning disabilities program. During the interview, the applicant can be asked questions to assess knowledge of basic concepts in English, math, and the physical and social sciences.

Can the applicant succeed in college? Program directors reported that oftentimes learning disabled students who are bright and knowledgeable found it difficult to succeed in college because they lacked other qualities that were important for college success. To obtain information about these qualities, the staff of most learning disabilities programs required a personal interview with each applicant. The interviews were sometimes conducted by the director or assistant director (Webb, communication, July 15, 1982), at other times by the learning disabilities program staff (Bireley & Manley, 1980) and in still other cases, by an admissions team composed of the program director, admission counselor, and a psychologist (Götz, communication, September 1982).

There was considerable agreement about the information to be sought during the interview.* Basically, an interviewer should look for: thinking ability characteristic of college students; an understanding of basic concepts in English, math, and the social and physical sciences; motivation to succeed in college; evidence that productive use was made of the high school years; an understanding of one's learning disability; an understanding of one's academic strengths and weaknesses; an understanding of how one learns; emotional maturity and stability; evidence of assertiveness in acting as one's own advocate; an inquiring and questioning

*Vogel and Adelman, 1981; and personal communications with K. Chandler, June 9, 1982; I. Götz, September 1982; J. McGuire, October 1982; P. Quinlan, July 16, 1982; D. Saddler, July 14, 1982; and G. Webb, July 15, 1982.

mind; an awareness of the consequences of inappropriate behavior; an awareness of one's underachievement in college prerequisite skills; and self sufficiency.

Parents were often requested to accompany the applicant for a campus visit and interview. Most often, the applicant was interviewed in the absence of the parents. After the interview, a conference was held with the parents to verify the facts presented by the applicant and to obtain additional information. During the conference, staff members sought assurances that parents would fully support the goals of the learning disability program.

After the interview, the learning disabilities staff reviews the information to decide if the applicant could profit from the learning disability program and eventually graduate from the college. Once they make their decision, the program director forwards a recommendation to the college Director of Admission for action. The Director of Admission then notifies the applicant.

An examination of the preceding procedures clearly points out that the responsibility for implementing special admission procedures rests with the staff of the learning disability program. The flexibility shown by colleges in their admission procedures and the good working relationship between the learning disability program staff members and personnel in the Office of Admission has allowed many learning disabled students to gain admission to colleges. Admission is a long procedure, however, and program directors recommend that interested learning disabled students begin looking for a college with a learning disability program in their junior year of high school. While more and more opportunities are becoming available for learning disabled students to attend college, as Cordoni (1980) pointed out, there are still more learning disabled students trying to get into college than there are openings in well designed programs created to service them.

6

Diagnostic Testing

The information obtained for a student in the admission process, as described in Chapter 5, is important for determining whether the student has a learning disability and can be helped by the learning disabilities college program. Diagnostic testing is needed to assess cognitive ability, academic skills, language abilities, auditory and visual learning skills, personal and social characteristics, and work and study habits. Information is obtained primarily from standardized tests. Data obtained during the admission procedure is also used. Similarly, data available from reports of prior testing are used. Where necessary, informal testing is done to supplement the standardized testing.

It is important to complete diagnostic testing as early in a learning disabled student's college career as possible. In some programs, this was done during a summer session preceding the student's arrival on campus. In other cases, students were required to participate in one or two days of testing prior to beginning their classes. All the college learning disabilities programs we contacted arranged to have students tested no later than the end of their first semester.

The data from the diagnostic testing combined with other information, is used to formulate an individual education program (IEP) for each learning disabled student. The IEP is discussed in Chapter 7.

Most programs we contacted had psychoeducational diagnosticians to perform the testing, to score and interpret the tests, and to generate IEPs. In some cases, this was a function performed by the director or by the assistant director of the learning disabilities college program. Occasionally, specialized testing centers at a college or university were utilized. These included psychological clinics, counseling centers, speech and language centers, and reading centers. These specialized centers rarely existed at the small, private colleges in which some of the learning disabilities college programs were located.

There are several inherent difficulties in the diagnostic testing of learning disabled college students. There is an insufficient number of tests available with norms extending to college age. Many of the tests lack adequate validity and reliability. Many standardized tests do not yield specific information needed to plan IEPs. There are very few tests for assesing written language abilities, affective characteristics, social development, and work and study habits.

We found that there was no one set of tests that can be described as the standard diagnostic test battery for college learning disabilities programs. Because of individual differences in training and philosophy of staff members, each program developed its own test battery. Certain tests were used more frequently than others. We describe the 15 most frequently used tests in detail in this chapter. Less frequently used tests that can be used with college learning disabled students are listed in Table 6-1.

STANDARDIZED TESTS

What follows are the 15 standardized tests most frequently included in the diagnostic battery of learning disabilities college programs. The 15 tests are not distributed evenly across the 7 domains of characteristics we identified for learning disabled college students in Chapter 3. There are 5 frequently used tests in the academic area. On the other hand, there are no tests reported as frequently used in the written language, social, or work and study areas. Only one test was reported as frequently used to measure affective characteristics of learning disabled college students.

Frequently Used Standardized Tests

Comprehensive tests are described first, followed by tests measuring intelligence, academic skills, language abilities, perceptual skills, and affective characteristics.

Woodcock-Johnson Psycho-Educational Battery (WJPEB)

Authors.   Richard W. Woodcock and M. Bonner Johnson.

Publisher.   Teaching Resources Corporation, 50 Pond Park Road, Hingham, Massachusetts   02043.

Year of publication.   1977.

Abilities and skills tested.   Cognitive abilities, scholastic aptitudes, academic achievement, and scholastic and nonscholastic interests.

Age or grade range of norms. Age 3 to age 80 and older.

Testing time. 2 hours, 30 minutes to 3 hours.

Description. The Woodcock-Johnson Psycho-Educational Battery (WJPEB) consists of a series of cognitive, achievement, and interest subtests. The subtests within each part are as follows:

Cognitive Subtests

Picture Vocabulary. This subtest requires the subject to provide names for pictured objects or actions. The subject is shown plates with one to four pictures and is asked to name each picture. This subtest primarily measures expressive vocabulary skills.

Spatial Relations. The subject is shown a picture and is asked to select from a series of shapes those that are needed to make the whole figure. This subtest primarily measures visual and nonverbal processing skills. This is a timed subtest that measures the speed and automaticity of the subject's skills in the areas tested.

Memory for Sentences. This subtest requires the subject to repeat sentences that the examiner presents orally. The sentences become longer and more semantically and syntactically difficult as the items progress. This subtest measures both short-term auditory memory and expressive syntax abilities.

Visual-Auditory Learning. The subject is shown a series of rebus-like symbols and given their names. The subject is then asked to read various combinations of the symbols. The sequence of symbols become progressively longer, and the vocabulary becomes more difficult. This subtest is a visual-verbal learning test that is thought to simulate the learning-to-read process. It is designed to assess the ability to benefit from instruction and feedback as well as rate of learning.

Blending. This subtest requires the subject to blend isolated sounds into meaningful words. It is a measure of auditory synthesis ability. The number of phonemes increases as the test items progress.

Quantitative Concepts. This subtest requires the subject to answer questions related to quantitative and mathematic concepts, symbols, and vocabulary. It measures understanding of mathematic concepts, symbols, and vocabulary.

Visual Matching. This subtest requires the subject to identify and circle two identical numerals in a row of six numerals. The items increase in difficulty from single-digit to five-digit numerals. This is a timed

Table 6-1 Additional Standardized Tests

Name of Test	Grade or Age Level	Time	Publisher
Cognitive			
Leiter International Performance Scale	2–18 years	30–60 minutes	C.H. Stoelting
Ravens Progressive Matrices	6 years–adult	10–40 minutes	Psychological Corporation
Stanford-Binet Intelligence Scale	2 years–adult	30–90 minutes	Houghton Mifflin
Language			
Brown-Carlson Listening Comprehension Test	Grade 9–adult	Untimed	Lyons and Carnahan
Compton-Hutton Phonological Assessment	Preschool–adult	20–25 minutes	Carousel House
Fisher-Logemann Test of Articulation Competence	3 years–adult	25 minutes	Houghton Mifflin
Goldman-Fristoe Test of Articulation	3–16 years	20 minutes	American Guidance Service
Language Structured Auditory Attenion Span Test	3 years–adult	20 minutes	Academic Therapy
Myklebust Picture Story Language Test	7–17 years	20–30 minutes	Grune & Stratton
Templin-Darley Tests of Articulation	3 years–adult	25–30 minutes	The University of Iowa
PRO-Ed Test of Adolescent Language	11–18 years, 6 months	30–45 minutes	PRO-Ed
Perceptual-Motor			
Ayres Space Test	3 years–adult	20–30 minutes	Western Psychological Services
Benton Visual Retention Test	8 years–adult	5–10 minutes	Psychological Corporation
Goldman-Fristoe-Woodcock Auditory Skills Battery	4 years–adult	20–25 minutes	American Guidance Service
Lateral Awareness and Directionality Test	Grade K–12	15–20 minutes	Academic Therapy
Lindamood Auditory Conceptualization Test	Preschool–adult	10–15 minutes	Teaching Resources
Memory-For-Designs Test	8 years–adult	10 minutes	Psychological Test Specialists
Minnesota Manual Accuracy and Speed Test	Preschool–adult	30 minutes	Special Education Materials
MKM Auditory Letter Recognition Test	Preschool–adult	10 minutes	MKM
Oliphant Auditory Synthesizing Test	Grade 1–adult	5–15 minutes	Educator's Publishing Service

Test	Range	Time	Publisher
Slosson Drawing Coordination Test for Children and Adults	1 year–adult	10–15 minutes	Slosson Educational Publications
Standardized Road Map of Directional Sense Test	7 years–adult	Untimed	Academic Therapy

Academic

Test	Range	Time	Publisher
Botel Reading Inventory	Grade 1–adult	60–90 minutes	Follett Educational Corporation
California Phonics Survey	Grade 7–adult	Untimed	Consulting Psychologist Press
Clarke Reading Self-Assessment Survey	High school–adult	Untimed	Academic Therapy
Diagnostic Spelling Test	Grade 2–12	Untimed	CTB/McGraw-Hill
Diagnostic Tests and Self-Help in Arithmetic	Grade 3–adult	Untimed	CTB/McGraw-Hill
Diagnostic Word Patterns	Grade 2–college	15–20 minutes	Eductor's Publishing Service
Gates-MacGinitie Silent Reading Tests	Grade 1–12	50–60 minutes	Teacher's College Press
Lincoln Diagnostic Spelling Test	Grade 2–adult	50 minutes	Educational Records Bureau
Nelson-Denny Reading Test	Grade 9–adult	30 minutes	Houghton Mifflin
Reading Miscue Inventory	Grade 1–adult	15–20 minutes	Macmillan
Slosson Oral Reading Test	Grade 1–adult	3 minutes	Slosson Educational Publications
Spache Diagnostic Reading Scales	Grade 1–12	30–45 minutes	CTB/McGraw-Hill
Test of Everyday Writing Skills	Grade 7–adult	Untimed	CTB/McGraw-Hill
Tests of Academic Progress	Grade 9–adult	70 minutes	Houghton Mifflin
Traxler High School Spelling Test	Grade 9–adult	Untimed	Bobbs-Merrill
Traxler Silent Reading Test	Grade 7–10	46–53 minutes	Bobbs-Merrill

Work and Study Skills

Test	Range	Time	Publisher
Survey of Study Habits and Attitudes	Grade 7–14	20–25 minutes	Psychological Corporation

Affective

Test	Range	Time	Publisher
California Psychological Inventory	Adolescent–adult	45–60 minutes	Consulting Psychologist Press
Minnesota Multiphasic Personality Inventory	Grade 9–adult	30–90 minutes	Psychological Corporation
Weller-Strawser Scales of Adaptive Behavior	Grade K–12	Untimed	Academic Therapy

subtest that requires speed and fluency as well as the ability to identify and match numerals. It is basically a measure of visual-perceptual fluency and accuracy.

Antonyms-Synonyms. Part A of this subtest, antonyms, requires the subject to state a word whose meaning is the opposite of a given word. Part B, synonyms, requires the subject to state a word whose meaning is approximately the same as a given word. In each part of this subtest, the words become progressively more difficult. The subtest measures understanding of word meanings and expressive vocabulary.

Analysis-Synthesis. This subtest requires a subject to analyze the components of an equivalency statement and reintegrate them to determine the components of a novel equivalency statement. The subtest is designed to evaluate the subject's ability to learn symbolic formulations and then, using mental processing and reasoning, to apply them in problem-solving tasks. It evaluates higher-level, nonverbal learning and problem-solving abilities. As for the Visual-Auditory Learning subtest, this subtest measures the ability to benefit from feedback instruction.

Numbers Reversed. This subtest requires a subject to repeat a series of random numbers in reverse order. The items range from two-digit numbers to eight-digit numbers. This subtest measures short-term memory and perceptual reorganization.

Concept Formation. In this subtest, the subject is shown problems that contain examples and nonexamples of concepts and is required to determine the rule that applies. This subtest primarily measures nonverbal abstract reasoning abilities, especially as they are used in rule learning and logic. Along with the Visual-Auditory Learning and Analysis-Synthesis subtests, this subtest also measures the subject's ability to benefit from instruction and feedback.

Analogies. This subtest requires a subject to complete oral statements of verbal analogies. This subtest measures vocabulary, comprehension, conceptualization, and expression.

Achievement Subtests

Letter-Word Identification. This subtest requires a subject to name individual letters and read individual words. It is primarily a measure of sight-word vocabulary.

Word Attack. This subtest requires a subject to read phonetically regular nonsense words or words that are of extremely low frequency in the English language. The items begin with relatively simple consonant-vowel-consonant trigrams and progress to more complex single-syllable words and eventually, multisyllable words. This subtest measures the ability to employ phonic and structural analysis skills.

Passage Comprehension. In this subtest, the subject is required to silently read short passages and then to identify and supply missing key words. This subtest primarily measures literal reading comprehension skills.

Calculation. This subtest evaluates the subject's ability to perform mathematic calculations. Items range from simple operations to geometric, trigometric, logarithmic, and calculus operations.

Applied Problems. In this subtest, the subject is required to solve practical problems of mathematics. The items begin with simple counting tasks and progress to relatively complex calculation and mathematic operations. The items assess knowledge of money, measurement, time, probability, and geometry. This is basically a measure of mathematics reasoning ability.

Dictation. This subtest requires a subject to respond in writing to a variety of questions testing knowledge of letter forms, spelling, punctuation, capitalization, and language usage such as contractions, abbreviations, and plurals. It is a measure of spelling and also tests the use of punctuation and capitalization rules.

Proofing. In this subtest, the subject is presented with sentences each containing one error, and is required to identify the error. The errors include incorrect punctuation, incorrect capitalization, misspellings, and inappropriate grammatical use of words. This subtest assesses spelling, punctuation, capitalization, and word usage.

Science. In this subtest, the subject is required to respond orally to questions assessing knowledge of biologic and physical sciences.

Social Studies. In this subtest, the subject is required to respond orally to questions assessing knowledge of geography, government, economics, and other aspects of social studies.

Humanities. In this subtest, the subject is required to respond orally to questions assessing knowledge of art, music, and literature.

Interest Level Subtests

Reading Interests. In this subtest, the subject is required to respond to items indicating preference for participating in reading activities.

Mathematics Interest. In this subtest, the subject is required to respond to items indicating preference for participating in activities involving the learning or application of mathematics.

Written Language Interests. In this subtest, the subject is required to respond to items indicating preference for various forms of activities requiring written language.

Physical Interests. In this subtest, the subject is required to respond to items indicating preference for participating in individual and group physical activities.

Social Interests. In this subtest, the subject is required to respond to items indicating preference for participating in activities involving other people.

The WJPEB is a comprehensive test that measures many of the abilities and skills important to consider when developing an IEP for learning disabled college students. This test permits derivation of a variety of types of scores, some of which are unique to the test. There are many ways to interpret the test results. Because of the complexity of interpreting this test, we recommend that readers contemplating its use refer to the interpretation handbook developed by Hessler (1982). The WJPEB is a relatively new test that is gaining increased acceptance and use in education and psychology. We believe it has the potential to be a major instrument for use with learning disabled college students.

Detroit Tests of Learning Aptitude

Authors.   Harry J. Baker and Bernice Leland.

Publisher.   PRO-ED, 5341 Industrial Oaks Boulevard, Austin, Texas 78735. (Originally published in 1935 by Bobbs-Merrill Company, Inc., 4300 W. 62nd Street, Indianapolis, Indiana   46206.)

Year of Publication.   Examiner's Handbook revised in 1967.

Abilities and skills tested.   Reasoning and comprehension, practical judgement, verbal ability, time and space relationships, number ability, auditory attentive ability, visual attentive ability, and motor ability.

Age or grade range of norms.   3 to 19 years.

Testing time.   60 to 75 minutes (based on administering 9 to 13 subtests).

Description.   The Detroit Tests of Learning Aptitude (Detroit) contains 19 subtests measuring various aspects of intellectual functioning. The authors of the test recommend that from 9 to 13 tests be administered based on those abilities that the examiner is most interested in. A mental age score is obtained for each subtest. By dividing the median mental age score by the subject's chronological age, a ratio IQ is obtained.

Some of the Detroit Subtests may be used only with young children. We describe below only those subtests appropriate for older individuals and frequently used with learning disabled college students.

Verbal Absurdities. This subtest requires the student to listen to a statement and identify the illogical or erroneous cause-and-effect relationship. This subtest measures reasoning and comprehension, and verbal ability.

Verbal Opposites. This subtest requires the subject to name antonyms for sample words that gradually increase in difficulty. This subtest measures verbal ability.

Motor Speed and Precision. This timed subtest requires the subject to make Xs in circles that gradually decrease in size. This subtest measures practical judgment and motor ability.

Auditory Attention Span for Unrelated Words. This subtest requires the subject to remember and recall sets of pictures on cards, the pictures increasing in number from two to eight per card. This subtest measures visual attentive ability.

Free Association. This subtest requires the subject to say as many words as possible in a specified period of time. This subtest measures verbal ability.

Memory for Designs. This subtest requires the subject to copy geometric forms from a model, and/or reproduce them from memory after viewing them for a few seconds. This subtest measures time and space relationships, visual attentive ability, and motor ability.

Auditory Attention Span for Related Syllables. This subtest requires the subject to repeat sentences of increasing length and complexity. This subtest is a measure of auditory attentive ability.

Social Adjustment B. This subtest requires the subject to answer questions about civic affairs and common objects. This subtest is a measure of reasoning and comprehension.

Visual Attention Span for Letters. This subtest requires the subject to remember and recall sets of letters on cards, the letters increasing in number from two to seven. This subtest is a measure of visual attentive ability.

Disarranged Pictures. This subtest requires the subject to mentally rearrange pictures that are broken into sections. This subtest is a measure of reasoning and comprehension, time and space relationships, and visual attentive ability.

Oral Directions. This subtest requires the subject to remember and carry out sets of directions, the units increasing in number from two to five. This subtest measures practical judgment, auditory attentive ability, visual attentive ability, and motor ability.

Likenesses and Differences.   This subtest requires the subject to express similarities and differences between pairs of terms that gradually become more abstract. This subtest measures verbal ability.

The Detroit is a popular test because it measures a wide range of abilities, and in many cases does so in a unique, clinical manner. Its major limitations are insufficient information on validity, reliability, and norms, and the fact that the test was constructed approximately 50 years ago. Consideration is being given to revising the test.

Wechsler Adult Intelligence Scale—Revised (WAIS–R)

Author.   David Wechsler.

Publisher.   The Psychological Corporation, 757 Third Avenue, New York, New York   10017.

Year of publication.   1981

Abilities and skills tested.   General mental abilities.

Age or grade range of norms.   16 to 75 years.

Testing time.   60 to 90 minutes.

Description.   The WAIS–R is composed of 11 subtests, 6 verbal and 5 nonverbal. The verbal subtests yield a Verbal IQ, and the nonverbal subtests yield a Performance IQ. Administration of the total test yields a Full Scale IQ.

Verbal Section

Information. This subtest requires the subject to answer basic fact questions. This subtest measures a subject's range of general factual knowledge.

Digit Span. This subtest requires a subject to repeat a series of numbers in exact order. One part of this subtest requires a subject to repeat digits in forward order, with the number of digits in a set progressing from three to nine. A second section requires a subject to repeat digits in backward order, with the sets of digits progressing from two to eight. This subtest measures auditory short-term memory.

Vocabulary. This subtest requires a subject to define words. The words progress from concrete to abstract. This subtest measures a subject's language development and word knowledge.

Arithmetic. This subtest requires a subject to solve arithmetic word problems requiring mental computation. This subtest measures a subject's computational skill.

Comprehension. This subtest requires a subject to answer questions in which a judgment must be made about social situations. This subtest measures a subject's range of practical information and evaluation and use of past experiences.

Similarities. This subtest requires a subject to recognize likenesses between pairs of words representing concrete objects, substances, facts, or ideas. This subtest measures logical abstractive (categorical) thinking.

Performance Section

Picture Completion. This subtest requires a subject to identify a missing element in a picture. This subtest measures visual alertness and visual recognition and identification (longterm visual memory).

Picture Arrangement. This subtest requires the subject to put comic-strip picture sequences into a logical order. Items progress from three to five pictures. This subtest measures a subject's anticipation of consequences, and temporal sequencing and time concepts.

Block Design. This subtest requires the subject to reproduce designs made from colored blocks. This subtest measures a subject's ability to analyze a whole into component parts, nonverbal concept formation, and spatial visualization.

Object Assembly. This subtest requires the subject to assemble puzzle pictures of familiar objects. The puzzles progress from four to eight pieces. This subtest measures the subject's ability to benefit from sensory-motor feedback, anticipation of relationships among parts, and flexibility.

Digit Symbol. This subtest requires the subject to match numerals with specific symbols. The subject is required to write the correct symbol below each numeral. Like all other subtests in the Performance Section, this subtest is timed. This subtest measures a subject's ability to follow directions, clerical speed and accuracy, psychomotor speed, visual short-term memory, and motivation.

In addition to yielding a Verbal IQ, Performance IQ, and Full Scale IQ, the WAIS–R yields scaled scores for each subtest. These scaled scores can be used for differential diagnosis of learning difficulties.

Because the WAIS–R was developed in 1981, many diagnosticians continue to use the Wechsler Adult Intelligence Scale (WAIS). The WAIS–R and the WAIS are highly comparable. The changes in the WAIS–R basically involved revising or dropping dated items, adding some new items, modifying the scoring of certain items, and changing the order of the administration of the subtests. A great deal of information has accrued concerning the interpretation of the WAIS, and this information may similarly be used to interpret the results of the WAIS–R. The psychological literature contains many research reports of the performance of learning disabled persons on the WAIS.

Slosson Intelligence Test (Second Edition)

Author.   Richard L. Slosson.

Publisher.   Slosson Educational Publications, Inc., P.O. Box 280, East Aurora, New York   14052.

Year of publication.   1981.

Abilities and skills tested.   General mental ability.

Age or grade range of norms.   Young nursery school children to older adults.

Testing time.   15 to 30 minutes.

Description.   The Slosson Intelligence Test consists of a series of short-answer questions. No reading or writing is required of the subject. The test contains the following types of items:

Information. General fund of knowledge, longterm memory from experiences and education.

Comprehension. Practical knowledge of everyday experiences, logical solutions and common sense.

Arithmetic. Concentration, arithmetic reasoning, ability to utilize abstract concepts of numbers.

Similarities and Differences. Abstraction and concept formation skills, relationship and association of abstract ideas.

Vocabulary. Expressive language, word knowledge, verbal fluency.

Digit Span. Concentration, immediate auditory sequencing, rote memory.

Auditory Memory of Sentences. Concentration, auditory memory of meaningful materials.

Visual-Motor. Eye-hand coordination, motor control, visual-motor integration. (*Item Analysis of Slosson Intelligence Test for Children and Adults*, 1978).

The items selected for the Slosson Intelligence Test are similar in nature to those found in the Stanford-Binet Intelligence Scale. The test yields a Mental Age and IQ. Research with this test has generally shown that IQ scores are higher for normal and gifted subjects, but are slightly lower for below normal subjects. The test is best viewed as a screening test to be used by professionals who are relatively untrained in individual testing. It should not be used where an in-depth intellectual assessment is needed.

Peabody Individual Achievement Test (PIAT)

Authors. Lloyd M. Dunn and Frederick C. Markwardt, Jr.

Publisher. American Guidance Service, Inc., Publisher's Building, Circle Pines, Minnesota 55014.

Year of publication. 1970.

Abilities and skills tested. Mathematics, reading, spelling, and general achievement.

Age or grade range of norms. Grades K to 12.

Testing time. 30 to 40 minutes.

Description. The PIAT consists of five subtests. No writing is involved on this test. A subject's performance may be interpreted on the basis of either grade scores or age scores. The five subtests are:

Mathematics. This subtest presents questions ranging from matching numbers to algebra and geometry. The questions are read to the subject, who is required to select the answer from four visually-presented choices. All computation must be done mentally.

Reading Recognition. Initial items of this subtest measure readiness skills such as letter matching and letter naming. The remaining items are single words that the subject reads aloud.

Reading Comprehension. In this subtest, the subject is presented with a page that contains one sentence that is to be read silently. The subject is then shown a second page containing four pictures, and is required to select the picture that best illustrates the meaning of the sentence just read.

Spelling. Initial items of this subtest measure readiness skills such as finding the *different* symbol in a group of four, and letter recognition. The remaining items require the subject to select the correct spelling of a word pronounced by the examiner from four choices seen on a page. This subtest does not require actual written spelling.

General Information. This subtest requires the subject to answer questions whose content includes science, social studies, fine arts, and sports.

The PIAT is intended as a means of quickly establishing a student's levels of academic skills, and is not a comprehensive diagnostic instrument for any of the areas measured. Some learning disabled students have difficulty with the mathematics and spelling subtests because of their nonwriting format. Scores of such students on these subtests may therefore be depressed. The Reading Comprehension subtest presents picture response choices of considerable visual complexity at the higher levels, and this may be difficult for learning disabled students with deficits in the visual perception area.

Wide Range Achievement Test (WRAT)

Authors.   J.F. Jastak, S.R. Jastak, and S.W. Bijou.

Publisher.   Jastak Associates, Inc., 1526 Gilpin Avenue, Wilmington, Delaware   19806.

Year of publication.   1978.

Abilities and skills tested.   Reading, spelling, and arithmetic.

Age or grade range of norm.   5 years to adult.

Testing time.   20 to 30 minutes.

Description.   The WRAT is divided into two levels. Level I is designed for use with children between the ages of 5 and 12. Level II is intended for use with persons from age 12 to adulthood. Scores are interpreted on the basis of grade levels. For subjects ages 18 and 19 (the most likely age of the learning disabled college students who will be tested) the highest obtainable grade equivalents are: Reading 13.7, Spelling 13.1, Arithmetic 16.8. The three subtests of the WRAT are:

Reading. Level II requires a subject to pronounce individual words out of context.

Spelling. Level II requires a subject to write single words to dictation.

Arithmetic. Level II requires a subject to perform written computations.

The WRAT is the most widely used brief measure of basic academic skills. Its wide age range applicability makes it particularly attractive. It should be used to obtain an initial estimate of a student's basic academic skills rather than as a diagnostic assessment of these skills. Two of the subtests are limited in format. The Reading subtest does not measure reading comprehension, a serious shortcoming when using the test with learning disabled college students. The Arithmetic subtest is a computation subtest that does not give information on a subject's ability to solve word problems and to reason mathematically.

Woodcock Reading Mastery Tests

Author.   Richard W. Woodcock.

Publisher.   American Guidance Service, Inc., Publisher's Building, Circle Pines, Minnesota   55014.

Year of publication.   1973.

Abilities and skills tested.   Varied reading skills.

Age or grade range of norms.   Grades K through 12.

Testing time.   30 to 45 minutes.

Description.   The Woodcock Reading Mastery Tests consist of five reading subtests. Two equivalent forms are available. The five subtests are:

Letter Identification. This subtest requires the subject to name letters of the alphabet. A variety of common letter forms in upper and lower case, and manuscript and cursive are presented.

Word Identification. This subtest requires the subject to read individual words aloud.

Word Attack. This subtest requires the subject to pronounce nonsense words using phonic and structural analysis skills.

Word Comprehension. This subtest requires the subject to read three words silently and then provide a word to complete an analogy.

Passage Comprehension. This subtest requires the subject to read a one- or two-sentence passage and then provide an appropriate word to fill in a blank. This is known as a CLOZE format.

The Woodcock Reading Mastery Tests yield a variety of scores. These include grade level scores, reading range, an achievement index, relative mastery scores, and percentile ranks. Modified norms are available for students performing above grade level 12.9. Some learning disabled students may have difficulty with the process of verbal analogies on the Word Comprehension Test, and the CLOZE technique used in the Passage Comprehension subtest.

Gray Oral Reading Tests

Author. William S. Gray.

Publisher. Bobbs-Merrill Company, Inc., 4300 West 62nd Street, Indianapolis, Indiana 46206.

Year of publication. 1967.

Abilities and skills tested. Oral reading.

Age or grade range of norms. Grades 1 to college.

Testing time. 15 to 20 minutes.

Description. The Gray Oral Reading Tests consist of four equivalent forms, each of which require a subject to read passages aloud. Each passage is timed, and is followed by four comprehension questions that are read to the student and answered orally. The passages cover the range from preprimer to adult reading. They become increasingly more complex on the basis of use of higher-level vocabulary, longer words, longer and more complex sentences, and higher-level concepts.

The Gray Oral Reading Test yields grade equivalents. The subject's speed of reading is an important determinant in the grade equivalent obtained. The test thus measures both accuracy and speed of reading. The examiner records the errors that a subject makes. These are coded into the following eight categories: aid (the examiner tells the subject the word after a five second hesitation by the subject), gross mispronounciation, partial mispronounciation, omission of word or phrase, insertion of word or phrase, substitution of one word for another, repetition of one or more words, and changes in word order. The comprehension questions give a measure of the subject's comprehension of literal meaning and immediate recall of facts. The subject's level of reading comprehension, however, does not affect the grade equivalent obtained on the test.

KeyMath Diagnostic Arithmetic Test (KeyMath)

Authors. Austin J. Connolloy, William Nachtman, and E. Milo Pritchett.

Publisher. American Guidance Service, Inc., Publisher's Building, Circle Pines, Minnesota 55014.

Year of publication. 1971.

Abilities and skills tested. Variety of mathematics skills.

Age or grade range of norms. Preschool to grade 8.

Testing time. 30 to 45 minutes.

Description. The KeyMath consists of 14 untimed subtests grouped into 3 major areas. Subtests in the Content area measure basic mathematic concepts and knowledge essential to an understanding and practical application of the number system. Subtests in the Operation area measure basic computational processes. Subtests in the Application area measure the subject's functional use of mathematics.

Content Area

Numeration. This subtest requires the subject to state an answer when given a picture, numeral, or diagram, and an oral question.

Fractions. This subtest requires the subject to state an answer when given a picture, numeral, or diagram, and an oral question.

Geometry and Symbols. This subtest requires the subject to point to the correct shape when given a picture of geometric shapes and an oral question.

Operations

Addition. This subtest has two types of items. In one, the subject is required to tell the correct answer when given a picture and an additional question. In the second, the subject is required to write the correct answer when given a written computation problem.

Subtraction. Same format as Addition.

Multiplication. Same format as Addition.

Division. Same format as Addition.

Mental Computation. This subtest requires the subject to tell the answer when given a computation problem orally.

Numerical Reasoning. This subtest requires the subject to tell what number(s) are missing when given a written arithmetic problem with missing number(s) and an oral question.

Applications

Word Problems. This subtest requires the subject to tell the answer when given a picture or printed material, and a word problem.

Missing Elements. This subtest requires the subject to tell what information is missing when given a picture or printed material, and a word problem.

Money. This subtest requires the subject to tell the correct answer when given a picture or diagram about money and an oral question.

Measurement. This subtest requires the subject to tell the answer when given a picture and a verbal question about measurement.

Time. This subtest requires the subject to tell the answer when given a picture and/or oral question about time.

The KeyMath yields an overall grade equivalent. In addition, a general pattern may be identified based upon the subject's performance in the three major areas of the test. The Appendix of the manual contains a description of each item, stated as behavioral objectives.

Although the norms for the KeyMath extend to the 8.8 grade level, the number of students in the standardization sample at the junior high school level is small. The test authors thus suggest the test as useful for preschool through grade six. There are items on the test, however, that extend to the ninth grade level of difficulty. The KeyMath is only useful for learning disabled students of college age who have very limited math skills.

Peabody Picture Vocabulary Test—Revised (PPVT)

Author. Lloyd M. Dunn.

Publisher. American Guidance Service, Inc., Publisher's Building, Circle Pines, Minnesota   55014.

Year of publication.   1981.

Abilities and skills tested.   Receptive vocabulary.

Age or grade range of norms.   Ages 2 years, 6 months to 40 years.

Testing time.   10 to 20 minutes.

Description.   The PPVT consists of 175 test items arranged in order of increasing difficulty. Each item has four simple black-and-white illustrations arranged in a multiple-choice format. The subject's task is to select the picture considered to best illustrate the meaning of an orally presented stimulus word.

Two forms of the PPVT are available. Each form allows derivation of standard score equivalents, percentile ranks, stanines, and age equivalents. Although raw scores are converted to age-referenced norms, grade-referenced derived scores are available from the publisher upon request.

Malcomesius Specific Language Disability Test

Author.   Neva Malcomesius.

Publisher.   Educator's Publishing Service, Inc., 75 Moulton Street, Cambridge, Massachusetts   02188.

Year of publication.   1967.

Abilities and skills tested.   Auditory, visual, and kinesthetic skills.

Age or grade range of norms.   Grades 6 to 8.

Testing time.   90 minutes.

Description.   The Malcomesius Specific Language Disability Test is an unnormed test that is an upward extension of the Slingerland Screening Tests for Identifying Children With Specific Language Disability. The test contains ten subtests:

Paragraph Copying. This subtest requires the subject to copy paragraphs from a wall chart.

Near Point Copying. This subtest requires the subject to copy a list of words in the test booklet.

Visual Discrimination. This subtest requires the subject to match visually similar words.

Visual Perception Recall. This subtest requires the subject to identify correct words and number sequences presented visually.

Visual Kinesthetic Recall. This subtest requires the subject to write phrases after a visual presentation.

Auditory Discrimination. This subtest requires the subject to discriminate words that sound very much alike.

Auditory Kinesthetic Memory. This subtest requires the subject to write phrases from dictation.

Auditory-Visual Integration. This subtest requires the subject to listen to a word or sequence of numbers and then select it from four similar choices presented visually.

Comprehension. This subtest requires the subject to listen to a paragraph and then write it.

Spelling-Auditory to Motor. This subtest requires the subject to write a list of 20 dictated words. Scoring of this subtest focuses on sound-symbol association rather than correct spelling.

The Malcomesius Specific Language Disability Test has three major disadvantages when used with learning disabled college students. First, it lacks norms. Second, the age range for which it is intended falls considerably short of college age. Third, this test does not yield a score. Detailed guidelines for evaluating test performance are presented in the test manual. A skilled clinician is able to use this test to informally learn about a subject's perceptual-motor abilities and learning style.

Goldman-Fristoe-Woodcock Test of Auditory Discrimination (GFW)

Authors.   R. Goldman, M. Fristoe, and R. Woodcock.

Publisher.   American Guidance Service, Inc., Publisher's Building, Circle Pines, Minnesota   55014.

Year of Publication.   1970.

Abilities and skills tested.   Speech-sound discrimination.

Age or grade range of norms.   40 to 70 years and over.

Testing time.   20 to 25 minutes.

Description.   In the GFW, a subject is presented a series of test plates, each of which contains four black-and-white line drawings representing words. One of the pictures represents the stimulus word, while the other three represent foils. The stimulus word differs from the foils by only one or two features including voicing, nasality, and manner of production. A test tape is used to present the stimulus words. The subject is required to listen to the word and then to point to a picture on a plate representing that word.

There are two subtests, each consisting of 30 test plates. One is the *Quiet* subtest in which the stimulus words are presented with no background noise. The second is a *Noise* subtest in which stimulus words are presented with background noise consisting of typical cafeteria sounds. The noise intensity is gradually increased on this subtest.

The GFW has several advantages over other tests of auditory discrimination. One is that its age norms extend into adulthood. The second is that the use of a test tape provides control of the examiner's voice. A third positive feature is a training procedure that ensures familiarity with the vocabulary. There is an error analysis matrix on the response form that allows the examiner to analyze errors according to distinctive features.

Bender Visual Motor Gestalt Test (Bender)

Author. Lauretta Bender.

Publisher. The American Orthopsychiatric Association, Inc., 1775 Broadway, New York, New York 10019.

Year of publication. 1938.

Abilities and skills tested. Visual-motor integration and emotional adjustment.

Age or grade range of norms. 5 to 11 years (Koppitz Scoring System); and 15 to 50 years (Pascal and Suttell Scoring System).

Testing time. 10 minutes.

Description. The Bender consists of a series of nine abstract designs to be copied by the subject. Each design is printed on a 4-by-6 inch card, and the cards are presented one at a time. The subject copies each design with the sample in front of him or her. There is a modification of the test that requires the subject to recall the designs from memory after initially copying them.

The Bender yields an age level score. There are a number of scoring systems available. Of particular interest in the case of college learning disabled students is the Pascal-Suttell scoring system (Pascal and Suttell,

1951). Average mean scores for men and women with college educations are presented by these authors. Pascal and Suttell viewed deviations of the execution of Bender drawings as reflecting disturbances in cortical functions, whether of a functional or organic basis.

Regardless of the scoring system that is used, the reality remains that most 10-year-old subjects can copy the Bender designs without any difficulty. Scores are thus meaningful for college learning disabled students only if they have a severe lag in perceptual-motor development. While the Bender can yield emotional indicators, this is dependent upon considerable clinical psychological expertise on the part of the examiner. The major limitation of this test with respect to the college age learning disabled student is the Bender's ceiling effect. It is possible that a college learning disabled student may have difficulties in the perceptual-motor area, but not of the magnitude that would be sensitive to this test.

Beery-Buktenica Developmental Test of Visual-Motor Integration (VMI)

Authors. Keith E. Beery and Norman Buktenica.

Publisher. Follett Publishing Company, 1010 West Washington Boulevard, Chicago, Illinois 60607.

Year of publication. 1967.

Abilities and skills tested. Visual-motor integration.

Age or grade range of norms. 2 to 15 years.

Testing time. 10 to 15 minutes.

Description. The VMI consists of 24 geometric forms that the subject is required to copy. The forms are arranged from the simplest to the most complex, and the subject may not erase or cross out anything that he or she draws. The raw score consists of the total number of forms copied correctly before the ceiling is reached, and this is converted to an age equivalent. In contrast to the Bender, where the subject copies designs on a separate sheet of paper, the VMI requires the subject to copy each form in a space provided below the stimulus form. The advantage of the VMI over the Bender for use with college learning disabled students is that the difficulty level of the stimulus forms extends to a higher developmental age level.

Tennessee Self Concept Scale

Author. W.H. Fitts.

Publisher. Counselor Recordings and Tests, Box 6184—Acklen Station, Nashville, Tennessee 37212.

Year of publication. 1965.

Abilities and skills tested. Self concept.

Age or grade range of norms. Age 12 years or higher.

Testing time. 10 to 20 minutes.

Description. The Tennessee Self Concept Scale consists of 100 self-descriptive statements that the subjects use to portray their own self-picture. It is a self-administered test. The Scale is available in two forms, a Counseling Form and a Clinical and Research Form. Both forms use the same test booklet and test items. The forms use different scoring and profiling systems. The Counseling Form is quicker and easier to score.

Staff of college learning disabilities programs who use the Tennessee Self Concept Scale as part of their diagnostic battery typically use the Counseling Form. The Counseling Form yields the following scores:

The Self-Criticism Score (SC). This score indicates whether the respondent is defensive or has normal openness and capacity for self-criticism.

The Positive Scores (P). There are nine different P scores:

Total P Score. This is the most important single score on the Counseling Form. It reflects the respondent's overall level of self esteem.

Identity. This score describes how the individual sees himself or herself.

Self Satisfaction. This score reflects the respondent's level of self satisfaction or self acceptance.

Behavior. This score measures the respondent's perception of his or her own behavior or the way he or she functions.

Physical Self. This score reflects the respondent's view of his or her body, state of health, physical appearance, skills, and sexuality.

Moral-Ethical Self. This score describes the self from a moral-ethical frame of reference.

Personal Self. This score reflects the respondent's sense of personal worth, his or her feeling of adequacy as a person, and self-evaluation of his or her personality.

Family Self. This score reflects the respondent's feelings of adequacy, worth and value as a family member.

Social Self. This score reflects the respondent's sense of adequacy and worth in his or her social interaction with other people in general.

The Variability Scores (V). The V scores provide a measure of the amount of variability, or inconsistency, from one area of the respondent's perceptions to another.

The Distribution Score (D). This score mesures the certainty with which one views himself or herself.

The Time Score. This score is simply a measure of the time the respondent requires to complete the Scale.

The Tennessee Self Concept Scale is easy to use and provides a wide range of scores. It is therefore widely used as a component of the diagnostic battery for college learning disabled students. The Scale is subject to the usual limitations of self-response type inventories in which the respondent may attempt to answer the questions in a way that he or she feels will please the examiner.

Less Frequently Used Tests

There are additional standardized tests that may be useful as part of the diagnostic battery used with learning disabled college students. These are listed in Table 6-1. For those readers interested in learning more about these tests, or identifying other tests, detailed information is available in the following:

1. Compton, C. *A Guide to 65 tests for special education.* Belmont, CA: Pitman Learning, Inc., 1980
2. Mauser, AJ. *Assessing the learning disabled: Selected instruments.* (Ed. 3) Novato, CA: Academic Therapy Publications, 1981
3. McLoughlin, JA, & Lewis, RB. *Assessing special students.* Columbus, OH: Charles E. Merrill, 1981
4. Buros OK (Ed.). *The eighth mental measurements yearbook.* Highland Park, NJ: Gryphon Press, 1978

INFORMAL ASSESSMENT

The use of standardized tests may not provide all the desired infomation about a learning disabled college student needed by the staff of programs for their diagnostic planning efforts. Program staff often use informal assssment techniques to supplement information from standardized tests. Guerin and Maier (1983) emphasize the value of informal assessment. They note that information gathered through observations of student behavior, examination of student products, and discussion with students provide the basis for sound instructional planning.

An examination of the standardized tests frequently used by learning disabilities college programs reveals that certain important areas of student functioning are not well represented. Underrepresented areas include written language, affective, social, and work and study habits. It is important, therefore, to use informal assessment techniques to gain information about the student in these areas of functioning.

Writing

In most learning disabilities college programs, students were required to provide a writing sample. In some cases, this was part of the admission process. An applicant was often required to write an autobiographic statement as part of the application procedure. Applicants were instructed to do this on their own and to produce the sample in their handwriting rather than in typewritten form. This allowed staff of the learning disabilities program to evaluate not only the applicant's ability to write effectively in a thematic sense, but also allowed analysis of handwriting mechanics.

Vogel and Moran (1982) discussed procedures for scoring expository essays of learning disabled college students on a holistic basis and on an analytic basis. The holistic scoring yields subscores in the areas of mechanics, organization, development, and style, as well as a total score that is a sum of these four subscores. The analytic scoring procedure provides an in-depth analysis of writing skills by assessing mechanics, spelling conventions, complexity and variety of sentence structure, complexity of T-units (minimal terminable units—main clauses), and word selection.

Guerin and Maier (1983) suggest analyzing written language for the following:

Productivity. This involves evaluation of the number of words, sentences, and words per sentence.

Sentence structure. This involves determination of whether the student uses well-formulated sentences. Guerin and Maier (1983) specify the following elements to be analyzed: subject and predicate agreement; complexity of sentences; run-on sentences; word order; word omissions; agreement in tense, number, and gender; variety in sentence structure; and amount of information in a sentence.

Punctuation. This involves a general impression of the adequacy of the student's use of punctuation.

Form.   This involves determining the student's ability to shift writing style depending on the needs. An examination should be made of creative writing, written reports, and correspondence.

Ability to abstract.   This involves evaluation of how the student transfers concepts of oral language into a written format. Guerin and Maier (1983) recommend specific assessment of: creative and varied use of vocabulary; logical or coherent development of a paper; elaborations used to support or explain points; major theme; development of minor points; use of summation, conclusions, and predictions; ability to construct a plot; and use of allegory, metaphor, and other figurative language.

Spelling.   The question here is whether spelling is sufficient for effective communication.

Self-correction.   Of concern here is the student's ability to monitor and proofread written work and to correct errors.

Handwriting.   Here the basic question is whether the handwriting is legible. We have found that the legibility of a student's handwriting can be determined by judging a relatively small set of characteristics. We ask the following questions as we evaluate a student's handwriting sample: Are there any letter distortions? Is the size of letters appropriate? Is the size of letters consistent? Does the student close letters such as *a, e,* and *o*? Does the student open letters such as *h, u,* and *w*? Is there appropriate space between letters? Is there appropriate space between words? Are letters and words oriented to the lines on the paper? Is there consistent use of manuscript or cursive within the same paper? Is there appropriate use of lower-case and upper-case letters? Is there a consistent slant when cursive writing is used? Are margins uniform? Is the speed of writing efficient? Does the quality of writing hold up over a period of time? and, Are excessive erasures and cross outs made?

Affective and Social Characteristics

Many learning disabilities college programs require students to participate in one or two days of diagnostic testing before the student actually begins the program. Because not all of the time is taken up by the actual administration of tests, there is opportunity for program staff to interact with the student and to observe the student in an informal manner. Barbara Cordoni, director of Project Achieve at Southern Illinois University in Carbondale, told us how she learned a great deal about prospective students during informal interactions with them (June 21, 1982). A student's sense of independence, for example, could be judged by noting whether the student came to the campus alone or was accompanied by his or her parents. If the parents were there, Cordoni wanted to see if they attempted to control the situation or allowed the student to conduct his or her own affairs. Cordoni often accompanied the student to the cafeteria for meal breaks. While walking there, she noted how the student became oriented to the campus. At the cafeteria, she observed how the student made basic decisions, and whether the student appeared comfortable or was anxious and defensive. The way the student interacted with program student assistants gave some indication of social relationships. Informal discussions with the student would often bring out many important points about the student's goals, feelings about himself or herself, anxieties and fears, and characteristic ways of behaving. These are just several examples of how the staff of learning disabilities college programs may take advantage of natural situations to learn a great deal about a student's affective and social characteristics. This informal data should be combined with information provided by professionals who have previously worked with the student, and the standardized test information.

Work and Study Habits

Considerable information may be obtained in this area by simply talking to the student and asking key questions. We suggest asking the following types of questions. Does the student:

1. Keep a calendar noting due dates of assignments and dates of examinations?
2. Set aside specific times for studying?
3. Prefer to study alone or in small groups?
4. Underline material in textbooks?
5. Take notes on what was read?
6. Use an outlining system?
7. Keep separate notebooks for each subject?
8. Play the radio or television when studying?
9. Study best early in the morning or late at night?
10. Write initial drafts of papers and revise them, or simply write a final draft?
11. Do recommended readings and optional assignments?
12. Know how to locate books and reference materials in a library?
13. Own a dictionary, encyclopedia, or thesaurus?
14. Keep notes from previous semesters?
15. Have a particular area set aside for studying?

A written report must be prepared and include the tests administered, the results, interpretations, and specific recommendations. In addition, a test data summary form can be developed. The format of the summary form will depend upon the tests in the diagnostic battery. A test data summary form should minimally include identification information about the student, the names of the tests given, the dates they were given, and the scores obtained.

7

Developing an Individual
Educational Program

In most learning disabilities college programs, an individual educational program (IEP) is written for each participant. The purpose of an IEP is to specify the services that will be provided to a student. The IEP is based upon data derived from diagnostic testing and information gathered during the admission process. In most programs, IEPs are rewritten each semester.

College learning disabilities programs are not required to prepare IEPs for their participants. Public Law 94-142 requires that IEPs be prepared for exceptional students only through the high school level. Staff of college learning disabilities programs recognize, however, that the IEP is an excellent device for planning and monitoring services delivered to college learning disabled students. In Table 7-1 we present a model IEP form. The remainder of this chapter discusses each section of the form.

ACADEMIC AND LEARNING STRENGTHS

Those skills that are at or very near college level are referred to as academic and learning strengths. These academic and learning strengths should be listed in Section I of the IEP form. Academic and learning strengths for a student could, for example, be listed as: logical thinking, verbal abilities, math problem solving, basic math skills, and dealing with people. This information will be used by the program staff to: involve the student in activities that he or she can perform competently and therefore, through them, experience success, and assist the student to develop compensatory strategies.

Table 7-1 Individual Educational Program

Name of Student	Academic Rank
Semester	Program Major

I. Academic and Learning Strengths (list)

II. Academic and Learning Deficits (list)

III. Effective Learning Strategies to be Used by Student (list)

IV. Effective Teaching Strategies to be Used With the Student (list)

V. Remediation

Semester Goal:
  Objective:
  Evaluation:
  Objective:
  Evaluation:
  Objective:
  Evaluation:
Semester Goal:
  Objective:
  Evaluation:
  Objective:

Table 7-1 *(continued)*

Evaluation:
    Objective:
    Evaluation:
Semester Goal:
    Objective:
    Evaluation:
    Objective:
    Evaluation:
    Objective:
    Evaluation:

VI. Tutoring

Name of course _____
Frequency _____
Tutoring strategies: (list)

Name of course _____
Frequency _____
Tutoring strategies: (list)

Name of course _____
Frequency _____
Tutoring strategies: (list)

(continued)

Table 7-1 (continued)

VII. *Counseling*

Group ———— or Individual ————

Frequency ————

Objectives: (list) ————

VIII. *Special Courses* (specify course name and number)

IX. *Auxilliary Aids and Services*

Taped texts

(Title) ————	(Author(s)) ————	(Publisher)
(Title) ————	(Author(s)) ————	(Publisher)
(Title) ————	(Author(s)) ————	(Publisher)
(Title) ————	(Author(s)) ————	(Publisher)
(Title) ————	(Author(s)) ————	(Publisher)

Notetaker (specify course for which needed)

————————

————————

Other (list)

Signature of student ———— Signature of Developer of IEP ———— Signature of Program Director ————

Date ———— Date ———— Date ————

ACADEMIC AND LEARNING DEFICITS

Those skills that are significantly below college level are referred to as academic and learning deficits. The academic and learning deficits of a student should be listed in Section II of the IEP form. Academic and learning deficits for a student, for example, could be listed as: reading comprehension, notetaking, auditory short-term memory, punctuation of written work, and vocabulary. These deficits must be remediated or the student taught techniques for compensating for them.

EFFECTIVE LEARNING STRATEGIES TO BE USED BY STUDENTS

The IEP should be useful not only to those who work with the student but to the student as well. Suggestions to the student about how he or she might learn more effectively should be listed in Section III of the IEP form. The student might, for example, be advised to: read chapter summaries before reading a chapter, review vocabulary before reading and studying, take written notes on reading assignments, set time schedules for studying, join a study group prior to taking tests, and answer study questions at the end of each chapter.

EFFECTIVE TEACHING STRATEGIES TO BE USED WITH THE STUDENT

Section IV of the IEP form includes suggestions for faculty members who have the learning disabled student in their courses. Those strategies that can make their instruction more effective for the student are listed here. Suggestions might include: using a text that includes a summary and questions at the end of each chapter, providing lists of key vocabulary terms, weekly evaluations of the student's work, permitting the student a longer time to take tests, and using other than paper and pencil forms of evaluation of student's attainment.

With the student's permission, a copy of the IEP should be sent to each of the student's professors along with an accompanying memorandum explaining its use. A sample memorandum is shown in Table 7-2.

REMEDIATION

Section V of the IEP specifies ways to remediate the student's identified deficits. These deficits were listed in Section II of the IEP. The remediation section of the IEP includes semester goals, objectives for

Table 7-2 IEP Memorandum to Faculty Members

To:	*(name of faculty member)*
From:	*(name of program staff member)*
Subject:	*(name of student)*
Date:	

At the request of *(name of student)*, I am sending you a copy of an Individual Educational Program (IEP) we have developed for the student.

The purpose of this IEP is to specify the services that will be provided to help *(student's first name)* succeed in college.

Section IV of the IEP contains suggestions that may assist you in providing the most effective instruction for *(student's first name)*. These suggestions were obtained as a result of extensive diagnostic testing completed on *(student's first name)* by the program staff. If implemented, they will help *(student's first name)* achieve in your class. We are available to elaborate upon and assist you with the implementation of any of these suggestions. You may contact me at *(telephone number)*. My office is in room _____ of the _____ building.

Both *(student's first name)* and members of the learning disabilities program staff thank you for your assistance in making college a better experience for *(student's first name)*.

reaching the goals, and procedures used to evaluate attainment of the objectives. There are many formats for writing goals, objectives, and evaluations. We recommend the format developed by the Center for Innovation in Teaching the Handicapped (Semmel, 1979).

Semester goals are a general statement of where a student should be in a given area of educational need at the end of the semester. Each goal statement should consist of four parts: direction of desired change, area of need, projected level, and resources needed. There are three possibilities for the direction of change desired. There can be an increase, a decrease, or no change in the present level of behavior. The area of need refers to the skill or behavior that requires special attention. The projected level refers to where the student can be expected to be at the end of the semester for which the IEP applies. This can be expressed as a grade level or criterion level. The resources needed are those required to help the student reach the projected level. Resources can include specialists or other personnel, materials, or specialized methods.

An example of a semester goal is, "increase comprehension for specific details to tenth grade level by individual remediation sessions." The specific components of this goal are: *direction of desired change—* increase; *area of need—*comprehension for specific details; *projected level—*to tenth grade level; and *resources needed—*by individual remediation sessions.

Specific objectives consist of three parts: conditions, performance, and standards. The conditions are the circumstances surrounding the performance. These can include instructional setting, materials used, and specific method employed. A performance is specifically what the student is to do. The standard is how well the student is expected to do the task. The standard is sometimes referred to as the criterion. An example of a specific objective is, "given written paragraphs on a tenth grade level in which words are omitted, the student will use the context to fill in the words that would make sense in that context with 95 percent accuracy."

The components of this objective are: *conditions*—given written paragraphs on a tenth grade level in which words are omitted; *performance*—the student will use the context to fill in the words that would make sense in that context; and *standards*—with 95 percent accuracy.

It is necessary to state how each objective will be evaluated. The actual procedure used to test for attainment of the objective must be specified. There are various ways to determine if the objectives have been attained. These include: direct observation, standardized or criterion-referenced tests, informal assessments, and behavioral checklists.

We recommend that no more than three semester goals and three specific objectives for each goal be included in the IEP for each semester. Our experience suggests that remediation efforts become fragmented and lack intensity when directed toward too many goals and objectives.

•

TUTORING

Remediation represents relatively longterm effort to help a student overcome deficits. Tutoring, in contrast, represents on-the-spot assistance provided to students in courses that are difficult for them. Section VI of the IEP should specify each course in which the student will be tutored, the frequency of the tutoring (for example, two sessions per week, each session for one hour), and specific strategies that the tutor should use. If a student is tutored in biology, for example, a strategy for the tutor to use might be to require the student to write each unfamiliar biology term on a file card, to look up and write the dictionary definition of that term, and then rewrite the definition on the card in the student's own words.

COUNSELING

If counseling is to be provided, it should be indicated in Section VII of the IEP. It should be specified whether the counseling will be individual or group. The frequency of counseling sessions and their objectives also need to be specified. Examples of possible objectives for a student might be to help the student: make friends, control anxiety in new situations, and raise self-concept.

SPECIAL COURSES

Some college learning disabilities programs offer special courses for their students. Examples of special courses include fundamentals of written composition, effective study techniques, and learning how to learn. In some cases, these courses are for degree credit and may or may not count in the student's GPA. When these courses are required, they should be indicated in Section VIII of the IEP.

AUXILIARY AIDS AND SERVICES

All auxiliary aids and services to be provided to the student should be listed in Section IX of the IEP form. When taped texts are used, be sure to include for each its title, author(s), and publisher. When notetakers are provided, the courses for which the notetakers will be used should be listed. Any additional provisions should be indicated in the section labeled, Other. For example, a student may need a tape recorder for recording class lectures, or a proctor may be needed to administer untimed course examinations.

To assure a common understanding, we recommend that the IEP be signed and dated by the student, by the person who developed the IEP, and by the director of the college learning disabilities program. Each should retain a copy of the IEP, and a fourth copy should be placed in the student's program file. At a designated time, the IEP should be reviewed and revised for the next semester.

8

Academic and Program Advisement

When students arrive at college, they are assigned to academic advisors. Usually the advisors are members of the faculty in the departments, colleges, or schools where the students intend to major. Students who have not selected a major are assigned to academic advisors who are very familiar with the undergraduate programs.

Academic advisors help students select majors, plan academic programs, and select courses for each semester or term. The typical college advisor meets with each advisee once or twice a semester. While this advisement procedure may be adequate for non–learning-disabled student, it is not adequate for learning disabled students.

THE NEED FOR SPECIAL ADVISEMENT

Swan (1982*) and Cordoni (1980) identified the following six reasons why learning disabled students need more careful advisement than non–learning-disabled students.

Learning disabled students have a tendency to enroll in courses that are too difficult for them. They often underestimate the reading and writing requirements of courses and frequently overestimate their own skills and competencies.

Once learning disabled students find an instructor who understands their learning disability, they tend to take as many courses as possible with that instructor. They take the courses even though the courses do not fit into their program of study.

---

*Swan, RJ. *A counseling model for promoting academic success of learning disabled students at the university level.* Unpublished manuscript, California State University at Long Beach, 1982.

As academic demands increase, many learning disabled students become manipulative or begin to withdraw academically or socially. Some learning disabled students become overly dependent on other students in their courses. They pressure students for help with term papers and tests. They do this by eliciting sympathy for their learning disabilities. Other learning disabled students lose hope of passing their courses and virtually give up.

Learning disabled students' self-reports of what they are doing in courses often cannot be trusted. Advisors must monitor the students' progress carefully to ensure that they are attempting to meet all course requirements.

Learning disabled students do not seek out the services they need to overcome academic and social difficulties that arise in college. Even though course tutoring and counseling may be available, learning disabled students often do not avail themselves of these services. They need to be encouraged and even sometimes directed to use appropriate services.

Registration is often overwhelming, and learning disabled students frequently accept poor advice from well-meaning students and staff members rather than consulting their advisors. As a result, learning disabled students frequently end up with overly difficult course loads, courses that are out of their program sequence, or a schedule that is poorly planned with respect to time.

RESPONSIBILITY FOR ADVISING LEARNING DISABLED STUDENTS

The responsibility for advising learning disabled students should initially rest with a member of the college learning disabilities programs staff. We suggest this for the following four reasons.

Staff members of the learning disabilities college program have detailed information about the nature and needs of the learning disabled student. As advisors, they have access to a wealth of information accrued through the admission process of the learning disabilities college program. In addition, they have direct access to the data derived from diagnostic testing.

Staff members in the learning disabilities college program have extensive general knowledge about learning disabilities and the impact of these disabilities on college work and study.

Staff members have first-hand knowledge of the services and aids available to the student through the learning disabilities college program. This knowledge enables the advisor to plan academic programs mindful of the support services available to the student.

Staff members of the learning disabilities college program have a working knowledge of the common courses taken by most of the learning disabled students during their freshman and sophomore years.

Once a learning disability student enters the Junior year, we suggest that advisement responsibility be transferred to faculty members within various academic departments throughout the college or university. We suggest this for the following two reasons.

In most cases, students have completed their participation in the learning disabilities program by the end of their sophomore year. At this time, they are participating fully in the mainstream of the general college program and need the same kind of academic advisement as any student.

Advising at the Junior and Senior year levels requires considerably more technical knowledge than advising at the Freshman and Sophomore levels. Students in the Junior and Senior years are heavily involved in their major fields of study and require advisement from faculty members who know specific courses and sequences within majors.

The transfer of advisement responsibilities between the college learning disabilities program and academic departments should be a planned and cooperative venture. Meetings should be held between advisors from the learning disabilities program and academic departments to arrange for the transition of advisement responsibilities. The academic records of the students should be reviewed and the need for any special adjustments in the academic program discussed.

STRATEGIES FOR ADVISING LEARNING DISABLED STUDENTS

Here are eight strategies that will be helpful to advisors from college learning disabilities programs and academic departments, when advising learning disabled students.

Consider the student's learning strengths and weaknesses when planning an academic program. Most learning disabilities college programs conduct extensive diagnostic testing of students during their first semester on campus. These tests provide important information about intelligence, academic skills, oral and written language abilities, perceptual skills, work and study habits, and personality traits. This data should be used to select courses compatible with the student's profile of strengths and weaknesses.

Vogel (1982) presented several examples of how learning disabled students' academic programs were planned using information on learning strengths and weaknesses. Students whose major difficulties were in reading comprehension and rate were advised to take only one heavy reading course per semester. Students with deficits in fine motor coordination were not advised, for example, to take a course in ceramics. Students with visual memory deficits were not advised to take courses such as art history.

As much as possible, advisors should help learning disabled students select courses compatible with their strengths. For example, a student with strong visual-spatial skills could be advised to take an elective in drafting. A student with strong auditory ability could be advised to take a music appreciation course.

Control the number of courses the student takes in a term. A learning disabled student should be advised to take a reduced course load. There are two important reasons for this. The learning disabled student has to spend more time preparing and studying for a course than does the non–learning-disabled college student. Vogel (1982) noted that non–learning-disabled students usually spend two to three hours in preparation for every hour in class, while learning disabled students spend four to five hours in preparation for every hour in class. Second, the learning disabled student typically participates in remediation, tutoring, and counseling sessions not required of non–learning-disabled students.

Advisors must rethink their concept of what a normal course load is when working with learning disabled college students. Most directors of learning disabilities college programs suggest that these students take no more than four courses per semester. By taking courses during the summer, a learning disabled college student can graduate in four years without taking a full course load each semester.

Control the difficulty of the course load. Courses selected by students should be balanced for level of difficulty. Bireley and Manley (1980) recommended that in a four course load, learning disabled students take one course considered difficult, two courses of moderate difficulty, and one course of minimal difficulty. The difficulty level of courses can be determined by analyzing grades received by students and course completion rates.

Consider the frequency and length of course meetings. Vogel (1982) reported that the amount of material and rate of presentation affected comprehension and integration of information by learning disabled students. For example, students with longterm memory deficits did better in courses that met several times a week than in those that met once a week. This is because courses that meet frequently usually have shorter grading periods and tasks and tests are based on smaller amounts of information.

The number of minutes a class meets is also important. Students with attention deficits may find it difficult to concentrate in classes that exceed an hour.

Consider who is teaching a course. Wherever possible, advisors should help learning disabled students select courses taught by professors who possess temperaments and instructional styles that are implicitly helpful to learning disabled students. Advisors should look for professors who:

1. Support the goals of the learning disabilities program.
2. Understand or are willing to learn about the nature of learning disabled students.
3. Are committed to meeting individual needs of students.
4. Are willing to meet with students beyond class time.
5. Have reasonable expectations.
6. Exhibit patience when working with students.
7. Clearly state all course requirements.
8. Present material in an organized manner.
9. Provide structure.
10. Frequently review material.
11. Present material at a reasonable pace.
12. Are flexible regarding the format of examinations and time deadlines for assignments.
13. Are interested in how students perform tasks (process) as well as outcomes (product).
14. Provide consistent feedback.
15. Present information using techniques that enable the learning disabled student to learn through both auditory and visual modalities.

Advisors must be diplomatic when helping learning disabled students select appropriate professors. This is best done by emphasizing the positive rather than negative qualities of professors.

Consider the instructional technique used. Some instructors require students to gain most of their information through listening and reading. Other instructors provide hands-on laboratory experiences and extensive field work. An instructor may use a seminar format requiring each student to participate in extended discussions. In some cases, courses may be conducted primarily through the use of self-taught instructional modules. These variations represent further logistical factors that must be considered when advising learning disabled college students.

Encourage students to prepare for courses in advance. Vogel (1982) recommended that learning disabled students begin reading and studying material in advance of taking courses. Advisors should encourage learning disabled students to meet with their course instructors before courses actually begin. At these meetings, students should obtain reading lists and assignments. They should begin preparing for these courses during intersessions or over the summer.

Contract with the student.   It is important to monitor the academic progress of learning disabled college students. A contract, such as Table 8-1, signed by the student and advisor can be used for this purpose.

Table 8-1 Learning Disabilities Program Contract

I, *(name of student)*, understand that the purpose of this contract is to establish conditions that will help me succeed in my program of studies. As a participant in the learning disabilities program, I agree to:

1. *Attend classes regularly.* I understand that I am allowed one unexcused absence per course. If I exceed one absence, I must present my professor with a written statement by my advisor specifying the reason for my absence.
2. *Stay in close contact with my professor.* I understand that for a grade of C or lower on any exam, I am to schedule a conference with my professor within 48 hours after the exam has been returned to me.
3. *Meet all requirements of my courses.* I understand that when I cannot complete an assignment as specified or when required, I must schedule a conference with my professor before the assignment is due.
4. *Set aside sufficient time for study.* I understand that as a minimum I will need to spend at least one hour a day preparing for each course I am taking.
5. *Meet with my advisor on a regular basis.* The schedule of meetings will be determined by my advisor and me at our initial conference.

I understand that the above requirements are in effect for the duration of my participation in the learning disabilities program. I realize that my failure to comply with the terms of this contract will jeopardize my continued participation in the program. Further, I recognize that if at any time my advisor has evidence that I have not complied with these requirements, he or she will notify the director of the learning disabilities program. The program director, in consultation with my advisor and me, will determine appropriate actions concerning my status in the program.

I fully understand and agree to fulfill the requirement of this contract.

_____ (date) _____   _____ (date) _____
Signature of Student   Signature of Advisor

_____ (date) _____
Signature of Learning
Disabilities Program Director

Advisors may require learning disabled students to keep a log of class attendance. On this log, the student should indicate the class attended, the date of attendance, the preparation done for the class, and any assignments resulting from that class session. An example of a class attendance log is shown in Table 8-2.

Table 8-2 Class Attendance Log

Name of student ———————————— Name of advisor ————————————

Course Attended	Date	Preparation	Assignments

9

Remediating Basic Skills

Remediation efforts in college learning disabilities programs have two basic purposes. One is to improve students' achievement in basic skills as closely as possible to that level of achievement required for successful work in college courses. A second is to teach students compensatory strategies that will minimize the impact of their academic and learning deficits upon their attainment in college courses.

WHAT ACADEMIC AND LEARNING
DEFICITS ARE REMEDIATED

Virtually all students in learning disabilities college programs require some remediation. Academic and learning deficits that are most frequently the focus of remediation efforts in college learning disabilities programs include: reading, written language, mathematics, spoken language, and work and study skills. Students vary in the number of areas in which they require remediation and in the intensity with which this remediation must be provided. Vogel (1982) stated that a student's need for remediation depends on three factors: the severity of their academic and learning deficit(s); the level of proficiency in those academic and learning skills needed for success in the student's program of studies; and the student's desire to achieve.

For purpose of remediation the staff of learning disabilities college programs divide students' areas of deficit into subskills. They focus remediation on the following subskills.

Reading.   Word attack, vocabulary, comprehension, and rate.

Written language.   Mechanics, spelling, sentence structure, organization, and format for term papers.

Mathematics.   Problem solving and computation.

Spoken language.   Expressive language and receptive language.

Work and study habits.   Note taking, use of study strategies such as SQ3R (Survey, Question, Read, Recite, Review), outlining, time management, and test taking.

PLANNING AND IMPLEMENTING REMEDIATION

Remediation takes place through a process in which the staff of college learning disabilities programs identify skills requiring remediation, schedule remediation sessions, assign remediation specialists, provide remediation, and monitor students' progress.

Test to Identify Needs

In Chapter 6, we discussed diagnostic testing of learning disabled college students. Diagnostic testing provides information on students' academic and learning deficits. These deficits are recorded on an IEP along with the goals and objectives for remediation (see Chapter 7). Remediation specialists should use the goals and objectives to provide focus for their instruction, and as a guide for selecting materials and choosing instructional techniques.

Schedule Remediation Sessions

The remediation provided to students through the resources of college learning disabilities programs is sometimes done on an individual basis, and in other cases with small groups of three to four students. The major advantage of individual remediation is that a student receives more instructional time from the teacher than is possible in group remediation. Small group remediation is advantageous for several reasons. First, it is economical. Second, it provides some novelty for those learning disabled students who have a long history of one-to-one remediation. Many of these students are bored with individual remediation (Swan, 1982*). Third, as Webb pointed out in a communication on July 15, 1982, by working in small groups the students can learn from each other.

We recommend that remediation sessions be scheduled to meet at least two times a week. We have found that intensity and regularity are keys

---

*Swan, RJ. *A counseling model for promoting academic success of learning disabled students at the university level.* Unpublished manuscript, California State University at Long Beach, 1982.

to successful remediation with learning disabled students. Remediation sessions scheduled on a once-a-week basis lack sufficient intensity and regularity. There is too much intervening time between sessions, allowing for regression of skills and forgetting of information.

Length of the session is another factor to consider when scheduling remediation. We recommend that sessions be scheduled for 50 minutes. This gives the remediation specialist sufficient teaching time and is not so long that the student's attention and concentration will diminish. If the specialist is to conduct a series of remediation sessions over a period of several hours, the 50 minute session allows the specialist a 10 minute break after each session. This allows the specialist to mobilize energy and organize materials for the next session.

Remediation must be scheduled around students' college courses. If students work, this also must be taken into consideration. We recommend that remediation sessions be held during the day, Mondays through Fridays.

Who Does Remediation

Persons providing remediation to learning disabled college students must have two important characteristics. They must be skilled teachers, and they must know about learning disabilities. Ideally, remediation should be provided by certified learning disabilities teachers. At colleges and universities with learning disabilities teacher-training programs, advanced students may be used as remediation specialists. In this way, not only will learning disabled college students be helped, but the students in the training program will gain valuable experience. When this is done, it is important that professional staff of the learning disabilities college program supervise the conduct and progress of the remediation sessions with particular attention.

In some learning disabilities college programs, specialists are used to provide remediation in a designated area. A reading specialist, for example, may provide remedial reading, a language therapist language training, and a study skills specialist note taking and test taking skills. When these specialists are not certified in learning disabilities, they should be given a comprehensive orientation to learning disabilities by the staff of the learning disabilities college program.

Providing Remediation

Remediation is designed to ameliorate academic and learning deficits and to teach students compensatory strategies for coping with their learning disabilities. Remediation of academic and learning deficits must be focused upon individual needs and be intensive, systematic, and regular. We offer the following guidelines to assist staff of learning disabilities college programs as they work to raise students' levels of attainment in their areas of weakness.

Focus remediation on students' deficits.   Students may resist doing work in areas where they have difficulty. It is not unusual for students to attempt to manipulate remediation specialists into letting them do things during the remediation sessions that the students are "good at." The specialists must remain firm and use remediation sessions to directly attack the students' areas of weakness.

Provide remediation at students' level of functioning.   Students' levels of functioning in their areas of weakness are considerably below what is usually expected for students of college age. Remediation, however, must be provided at the students' level of functioning regardless of how low this may be. Remediation specialists working with learning disabled college students must accept the reality that some students will be achieving at levels as low as junior high school.

Include testing as well as teaching.   Testing in remediation involves the clinical use of teaching activities to continuously determine what students have or have not learned. Testing provides the basis for planning successive remediation sessions. For example, if a student demonstrates difficulty computing with fractions in one day's remediation session, this becomes an objective for the next day's session.

Provide small steps in a graduated sequence of learning.   The remediation specialist should break the sequence of learning into small graduated steps. This allows students to experience success and provides a foundation for subsequent learning. If a student has difficulty syllabicating words, for example, begin teaching by using two syllable words and gradually build to words of four and five syllables.

Gradually increase the difficulty level of the stimulus.   The remediation specialist should structure stimuli presented to students in such a way as to start with an easy stimulus and gradually work to more difficult stimuli. When remediating deficits in reading comprehension, for example, begin with relatively short passages and proceed to increasingly longer ones.

Gradually increase the difficulty level of the response.   The remediation specialist should structure the response required from students in such a way as to elicit easy responses at first and gradually work to more difficult ones. When remediating a deficit in memory, for example, the specialist should require recognition responses before requiring recall responses.

Pace remediation according to mastery of objectives.   The pace of remediation must be consistent with students' individual rates of progress. This may be accomplished by establishing a criterion level of mastery for each objective. Students should not be moved to the next objective in a learning sequence until they have achieved the criterion level for the present objective. The remediation specialist should not move a student to a more difficult level on the basis of the progress of a group or a predetermined period of time.

Build transfer into remediation.   Students should be helped to transfer what is learned in remediation sessions to use in courses. For example, a student who is taught to identify main ideas in a reading passage should be taught how to use this skill to highlight or underline key information in required course readings.

Restructure a task when students cannot master it.   When students are unable to successfully respond to a remediation task, the remediation specialist should restructure the task in some way. If the student is unable to answer a question about something he or she read, for example, the question may be rephrased by the specialist. Another technique the specialist can use is to provide additional cues. For example, when giving the student a mathematics problem the specialist might underline key facts. Or, the specialist may ask certain questions that lead the student to discover the correct response inductively. The last resort the specialist should use is to provide the correct response for the student.

Set reasonable expectations.   Remediation specialists must guard against having unrealistically high expectations for the progress of the students. Specialists must keep in mind that the rate of learning of the typical student they work with will be below that of the non–learning-disabled college student. Expectations must be sufficiently high to motivate students to progress, but not so high as to frustrate them.

Compensatory strategies.   These help students cope with situations that require learning abilities that for them are underdeveloped. Students are taught strategies enabling them to utilize their learning strengths and bypass their learning weaknesses. For example, the student with auditory strengths and visual-motor weaknesses is taught to use a tape recorder to record class lectures rather than take written notes. Or, a student with poor auditory memory is taught to write down important information he or she must remember. Useful guidelines for teaching students compensatory strategies follow.

Teaching students to recognize their strengths and weaknesses.   Learning disabled students often have an imprecise understanding of the nature of their learning disabilities. Frequently the results of diagnostic evaluations have been reported to parents but not to the students. The students may have been told that they have learning disabilities, but with little or no interpretation of what that means. Remediation specialists should explain and demonstrate to students how they have difficulty learning, and the conditions under which learning becomes easier for them.

Teach students to recognize when they have to use compensatory strategies. Students need to be taught how to differentiate between those tasks they can master in a conventional manner and those requiring them to respond nonconventionally. A student with an auditory memory problem, for example, needs to be taught to differentiate between listening requirements for which he or she has adequate memory and those for which he or she will have to take notes or use a tape recorder.

Teach students many compensatory strategies.   The more compensatory strategies that students have in their repertoire, the better they are equipped to handle the varied learning requirements of college. Students should be taught to use tape recorders to assist them in listening, coaching and rehearsing to assist them in speaking, typewriters to assist them in writing, recorded textbooks to assist them in reading, and mnemonic devices to assist them in remembering.

Teach students transfer of strategies.   Students should be taught that a strategy they successfully use to master one learning requirement may often be used to master other learning requirements. For example, a student who is taught how to use a file card system to remember dates and events in a history course may be shown how to use file cards to remember the definitions of new words and terms in a biology course.

Monitor Remediation Progress

A written record of remediation sessions should be kept by remediation specialists. This allows staff of the learning disabilities college program to review the progress of remediation for each student. We recommend that specialists complete a remediation log for each session. A suggested form for this is shown in Table 9-1 and is explained here.

The Remediation Log has an area for recording the name of the remediation specialist, the date, the time, and the names of the students attending the remediation session. The form may be used with one or more

Table 9-1 Remediation Log

Name of remediation specialist _____ Students attending session _____

Date _____

Time _____

Objective	Procedures and Materials	Amount of Time Planned	Evaluation

students. Each objective for a remediation session should be stated using the format for stating objectives described in Chapter 7. The procedure(s) used to have the student(s) attain the objectives, and the materials needed to implement the procedures should be stated as concisely and specifically as possible. The estimated time needed to accomplish an objective should be reasonable. The specialist should complete the evaluation section of the form as close in time to the end of the session as possible. In the evaluation section, the specialist can record such observations as, which students did and did not attain the objectives; the effectiveness of the procedures and any suggested changes; the usefulness of the materials and any suggested changes; whether the amount of time planned was adequate, too little, or too much; and recommendations for the next remediation session.

The Remediation Log should be kept in duplicate. One copy should be kept by the remediation specialist and the other turned in to the designated supervisor from the learning disabilities college program. We recommend these logs be kept in loose-leaf binders. This allows specialists to work with only those logs needed at a given time. The Remediation Logs should be reviewed by supervisors at designated intervals. We recommend that this be done on a biweekly basis. Conferences between specialists and supervisors should be held on an as needed basis. Successful procedures and effective materials should be shared at group meetings.

SELECTING AND ACQUIRING MATERIALS

A variety of materials are needed to provide remediation for learning disabled college students. Materials are needed in all areas in which these students have deficiencies, and should range in difficulty from junior high school up to college level. Rather than identify specific remediation materials, we present a procedure by which the staff of learning disabilities college programs may obtain, review, and evaluate materials, and select those most appropriate for their programs.

Getting Access to Materials for Review and Analysis

In order to review and analyze materials one must have either the materials or a comprehensive description of them. Some materials may be available for review in curriculum libraries at colleges and universities, or materials depositories maintained by public school districts. Stowitschek, Gable, and Hendrickson (1980) conducted a phone and mail survey of all known national material information sources. They found that materials and descriptions of materials useful with learning disabled individuals could be purchased and/or borrowed from the following sources:

1. National Center for Educational Media and Materials for the Handicapped (NCEMMH). Address: c/o NCEMMH Information Services, The Ohio State Univeristy, 356 Arps Hall, 1945 N. High Street, Columbus, OH   43210.
2. National Information Center for Special Education Materials (NICSEM). Address: University of Southern California, University (RAN) 2nd Floor, Los Angeles, CA   90007.
3. Handicapped Learner Materials Distribution Center (HLMDC). Address: Indiana University, Audio-Visual Center, Bloomington, IN 47405.
4. Educational Resources Information Center (ERIC). Address: Council for Exceptional Children, 1920 Association Drive, Reston, VA   22091.

Stowitschek et al. point out that publishers are also important sources of information about materials. They specify three sources of information from publishers: brochures, advertisements, and catalogs; demonstrations by publisher representatives; and convention exhibits. In Table 9-2, we provide a sample letter that can be used to obtain materials and/or descriptions of materials from publishers.

Table 9-2 Sample Letter to Publishers of Materials

Date _____

Name of Publisher _____

Address of Publisher _____

_____

Dear _____

As a professional staff member of the program for learning disabled college students at *(name of college or university)*, I am responsible for evaluating and ordering instructional materials. I am interested in knowing about materials you publish in the areas of reading, written language, mathematics, language development, and work and study skills. These materials may range in level of difficulty from elementary through high school levels. I am particularly interested in high interest, low level material that can be used to remediate skills deficiencies.

I would appreciate samples and descriptions of appropriate materials. Please furnish the name and telephone number of your representative in my geographic area, and have the representative contact me. Also please send me a copy of your most recent catalog.

Thank you for your assistance.

Sincerely,
(Name of person writing letter)
(Position)

Many publishers produce materials that are applicable for remediation efforts with learning disabled students. A list of these publishers is provided in Table 9-3.

When looking for materials, staff of college learning disabilities programs should examine the following books that list teaching materials for learning disabled adolescents:

1. Alley, G, & Deshler, D. *Teaching the learning disabled adolescent: Strategies and methods.* Denver, CO: Love Publishing Company, 1979
2. Goodman, L, & Mann, L. *Learning disabilities in the secondary school.* New York, NY: Grune & Stratton, 1976
3. Sabatino, DA, & Mann, L. *Handbook of diagnostic and prescriptive teaching.* Rockville, MD: Aspen Systems Corporation, 1982
4. Woodward, DM. *Mainstreaming the learning disabled adolescent.* Rockville, MD: Aspen Systems Corporation, 1981

Reviewing and Analyzing Materials

It is important to have a system for evaluating materials to determine which should be purchased and used with learning disabled students. Stowitschek et al. (1980) developed a Materials Review Form that is helpful for this purpose. We recommend the use of this form, which is reproduced in Table 9-4.

The Materials Review Form is divided into the following sections: Identifying Information, Costs, Time Involved, Other, Preparation, Physical Characteristics, Instructional Characteristics, and Field Test Results. The use of each section of the form is as follows.

Identifying information. Here the evaluator notes general information such as the name of the material, the publisher, its purpose, the subject area it is developed for, the age or grade level it is developed for, the comprehensiveness of the program, and the date reviewed.

Costs. Here the evaluator records initial cost, cost per student, replacement cost, and hidden costs.

Time involved. Here the evaluator estimates what will be required in scheduling and teaching time, how long it will take to complete the program, and how much daily teaching time is involved.

Other. Here the evaluator records the types of responses required of students, and the prerequisites needed to begin the program or manipulate any media it involves.

Table 9-3 Publishers of Materials Appropriate for Use With Learning Disabled Students

Academic Therapy Publications
20 Commercial Boulevard
Novato, CA   94947

Adapt Press
808 West Avenue North
Sioux Falls, SD   57104

Addison-Wesley Publishing
106 W. Station Street
Barrington, IL   60010

Adston Educational Enterprises
945 E. River Oaks Drive
Baton Rouge, LA   70815

Allied Education Council
P.O. Box 78
Galien, MI   49113

Allyn and Bacon, Inc.
470 Atlantic Avenue
Boston, MA   02210

American Book Company
50 W. 33rd Street
New York, NY   10001

American Guidance Associates
1526 Gilpin Avenue
Wilmington, DE   19899

American Guidance Service, Inc.
Publisher's Building
Circle Pines, MN   55014

Argus Communications
7440 Natchez Avenue
Niles, IL   60648

Barnell-Loft
958 Church Street
Baldwin, NY   11510

Behavioral Research Laboratories
P.O. Box 577
Palo Alto, CA   94302

Benefic Press
10300 W. Roosevelt Road
Westchester, IL   60153

Book-Lab, Inc.
1449 37th Street
Brooklyn, NY   11218

Borg-Warner Educational Systems
7450 N. Natchez Avenue
Niles, IL   60648

Bowmar/Nobles Publishers
4563 Colorado Boulevard
Los Angeles, CA   90039

Cambridge
888 7th Avenue
New York, NY   10019

Communications Skill Builders
815 E. Broadway
P.O. Box 42050-H
Tucson, AZ   85733

Continental Press
520 E. Bainbridge Street
Elizabethtown, PA   17022

Cuisenaire Company of America
12 Church Street
New Rochelle, NY   10885

Curriculum Associates
5 Esquire Road
N. Bellerica, MA   01862

Developmental Learning Materials
P.O. Box 4000
One DLM Park
Allen, TX   75002

Dormac
P.O. Box 752
Beaverton, OR   97075

Economy Company
P.O. Box 25308
1901 N. Walnut
Oklahoma City, OK   73125

Edmark Associates
P.O. Box 3093
Bellevue, WA   98009

Educational Activities, Inc.
P.O. Box 392
Freeport, NY   11520

Educational Development Laboratories
1121 Avenue of the Americas
New York, NY   11020

Educational Performance Associates
600 Broad Avenue
Ridgefield, NY   07657

Educator's Publishing Service
75 Moulton Street
Cambridge, MA   02138

Fearon Publishers, Inc.
6 Davis Drive
Belmont, CA   94402

Field Educational Publishers
2400 Hanover Street
Palo Alto, CA   94302

Follett Publishing Company
1010 W. Washington Boulevard
Chicago, IL   60607

Garrard Publishing Company
1607 N. Market Street
Champaign, IL   61820

General Learning Corporation
250 James Street
Morristown, NJ   07960

Ginn and Company
191 Spring Street
Lexington, MA   02173

Grolier Educational Corporation
845 Third Avenue
New York, NY   10022

Grossett and Dunlap
51 Madison Avenue
New York, NY   10010

Gryphon Press
220 Montgomery Street
Highland Park, NJ   18904

Harper and Row Publishers
10 E. 53rd Street
New York, NY   10022

D.C. Heath and Company
125 Spring Street
Lexington, MA   02173

Hoffman Information Systems, Inc.
5632 Peck Road
Arcadia, CA   91006

Hubbard Publishing Company
P.O. Box 104
Northbrook IL   60062

Human Sciences Press
72 Fifth Avenue
New York, NY   10011

Incentive Publications
P.O. Box 12522
Nashville, TN   37212

Laidlaw Brothers
Thatcher and Madison Streets
River Forest, IL   60305

Language Research Associates
Box 95
950 E. 59th Street
Chicago, IL   60637

Learning Concepts
2501 N. Lamar Boulevard
Austin, TX   78705

Learning Skills
17951-G Sky Park Circle
Irvine, CA   92707

J. B. Lippincott Company
East Washington Square
Philadelphia, PA   19105

(continued)

Table 9-3 *(continued)*

Love Publishing Company
1777 S. Bellaire Street
Denver, CO   80222

Lyons and Carnahan
407 E. 25th Street
Chicago, IL   60616

MacMillan Publishing Company
866 Third Avenue
New York, NY   10022

Mafex Associates
Box 519
Johnstown, PA   15907

Charles E. Merrill Publishing Company
1300 Alum Creek Drive
Columbus, OH   43216

Modern Curriculum Press, Inc.
13900 Prospect Road
Cleveland, OH   44136

Modern Education Corporation
P.O. Box 721
Tulsa, OK   74101

Numark Publications
104-20 Queens Boulevard
Forest Hills, NY   11375

Open Court Publishing Company
1039 Eighth Street
Box 599
LaSalle, IL   61301

Phonovisual Products
12216 Park Lawn Drive
Rockville, MD   20852

Pitman Learning, Inc.
6 Davis Drive
Belmont, CA   94002

J.A. Preston Corporation
71 Fifth Avenue
New York, NY   10003

PRO-ED
5341 Industrial Oaks Boulevard
Austin, TX   78735

Random House/Singer School Division
201 E. 50th Street
New York, NY   10022

Reader's Digest Services
Educational Division
Pleasantville, NY   10570

Research Press
Box 317760
Champaign, IL   61820

Frank Richards Company
324 First Street
Liverpool, NY   13088

Science Research Associates
155 N. Walker Drive
Chicago, IL   60611

Scott, Foresman and Company
1900 E. Lake Avenue
Glenview, IL   60025

Select-Ed
117 N. Chester
Olathe, KS   66061

Special Child Publications
4635 Union Bay Place, N.E.
Seattle, WA   98105

Special Education Materials, Inc.
484 S. Broadway
Yonkers, NY   10705

Special Learning Corporation
42 Boston Post Road
Guildord, CT   06437

Stanwix House, Inc.
3020 Chartiers Avenue
Pittsburgh, PA   15204

Steck-Vaughn Company
P.O. Box 2028
Austin, TX   78767

VORT Corporation
P.O. Box 11552-H
Palo Alto, CA   94306

C.H. Stoelting Company
1350 S. Kostner Avenue
Chicago, IL   60623

George Wahr Publishing Company
316 State Street
Ann Arbor, MI   41808

Teacher's Publishing Corporation
22 W. Putnam Avenue
Greenwich, CT   06830

Webster Division, McGraw-Hill
Manchester Road
Manchester, MO   63011

Teaching Resources Corporation
100 Boylston Street
Boston, MA   02116

Westinghouse Learning Corporation
P.O. Box 30
Iowa City, IA   52240

Troll Associates
320 Route 17
Mahwah, NJ   07430

Zaner-Bloser Company
612 N. Park Street
Columbus, OH   43215

Preparation. Here the evaluator assesses how much teacher training is necessary before teachers can use the material, and daily teacher preparation time.

Physical characteristics. Here the evaluator notes what types of media hardware are required, whether any materials need to be duplicated and by what method, and whether any extra materials are required. In this section the evaluator also judges safety factors and durability. A notation is also made as to whether students are required to use a particular sensory mode when working with the material.

Instructional characteristics. This section of the form consists of a group of subsections. When recording information in these subsections, the evaluator determines the format of instruction required when using the material, whether the material contains objectives and how well they are sequenced, the type of assessment built into the material, the nature of the reinforcement system to be used with the material, and how many adaptations will be required to use the material with target students.

Field test results. Here the evaluator records the results of any field tests that have been done with the material. Stowitschek et al. (1980) observed that less than one percent of available materials report field test information.

Table 9-4 Materials Review Form

Identifying Information:

Title _____ Subject _____ Date Reviewed _____

Publisher _____ Level _____   Scope: Comprehensive _____

Address _____   Across Skills _____

Brief Description _____   Single Skill _____

Costs: (see Chapter 4)

Initial cost _____ Comment (Are the cost
cost per student _____ factors within reason?) _____

Replacement cost _____ _____
portion consumable (%) _____
portion reusable (%) _____

Initial cost low: _____ _____

Replacement cost low? _____ _____

Hidden costs? _____

Preparation:

Initial preparation/training involved _____

Daily preparation involved _____

Preparing materials _____

Comment (Are you willing to expend the effort required?)
_____

Physical Characteristics:

Media/hardware required...... _____ Comment (Are there
available .... _____ prohibitive physical
obtainable .... _____ characteristics?) _____

114

Time Involved

Time to complete in program (estimated)
weeks ___ days ___

Daily time required
of teacher ___ of learner ___

Comment _____

Other:

Response(s) required in the material _____
Prerequisites required _____
Student ability to use media equipment _____
Comment (prohibitive learner prerequisite?) _____

nonobtainable............ ___
alternatives?............ ___
service warranty?............ ___
local service?............ ___
can get on loan?............ ___
requires special training?..... ___
Duplication required............ ___
  mimeo............ ___
  xerox............ ___
Extra materials required............ ___
  locate............ ___
  make............ ___
Sensory mode required
  visual............ ___
  auditory............ ___
  tactual............ ___
  olfactory/gustatory............ ___
Safety
  toxic............ ___
  nontoxic............ ___
Durability of manipulatives
  durable............ ___
  nondurable............ ___

(continued)

Table 9-4 *(continued)*

Instructional Characteristics:

Format

	Self Instruction	One to One Tutoral	Small Group	Group
Initial Instruction	—	—	—	—
Drill and Practice	—	—	—	—
Enrichment	—	—	—	—

Comment _____

Direct Teaching

Appropriate practice: all pupil work is appropriate —
some pupil work is appropriate —
no pupil work is appropriate —

Comment _____

Reinforcement: general instructions —
specific instructions —
none specified —

Comment _____

(Are you going to have to design and implement your own reinforcement?)

Prompting: errorless responding possible —
fading of prompts —
no prompts provided —

Comment _____

Planning

Objectives: specific — general — not stated —
Comment _____

(Do the stated or implied objectives match your intent for the materials?)

Sequence: complete — gaps — not determinable —
Comment _____

(Is the sequence thorough and in logical order?)

Redirection: can recycle — can vary instruction — no redirection specified —

Comment ___

Amount of adaptation required (number of characteristics) —

Measurement

Initial assessment: placement — pretest — no initial assessment —

Comment ___

Progress assessment: daily — weekly — summary chart or graph — none specified —

Comment ___

Mastery assessment: same as initial assessment — same as progress assessment — raw assessment — no mastery assessment —

Comment ___

(Are you going to have to supply another assessment?) —

Field Test Results:

Subjective
1. expert appraisal............... —
2. publisher testimonials .... —
3. teacher testimonials .... —
4. marketing research .... —
5. no field tests reported .... —
6. individual learner verification .... —
7. one group field tests (pre-post-tests) .... —
8. controlled study comparing one material to another .... —
9. controlled study comparing material to objectives (validation research) .... —

Objective
10. performance warranty .... —

Reprinted from Stowitschek, J., Gable, R., & Hendrickson, Jm. *Instructional Materials for Exceptional Children* Rockville, MD: Aspen Systems, 1980, pp. 335–336, by permission of Aspen Systems Corporation.

The completed Materials Review Form should be circulated to professional staff of the college learning disabilities program. Staff members should make a recommendation regarding purchase of the materials to the person responsible for ordering materials. Once materials have been obtained and have been used by remediation specialists, the effectiveness of the materials with college learning disabled students should be evaluated. We suggest the dynamic evaluation techniques described by Wiederholt and McNutt (1977) be used for this purpose. Dynamic evaluation techniques include the following.

Pre/post testing.   This technique involves administering a test prior to and after students have used an instructional material. Wiederholt and McNutt (1977) suggest the use of criterion-referenced tests to judge students' acquisition of the specific information or skills purported to be covered by the materials.

Analytic teaching.   This technique refers to those methods that allow the remediation specialist to analyze students' behavior while the students are using the instructional material. Of primary interest is how the material facilitates students' learning. The analytic teaching technique requires that: students must be systematically observed using the materials, students' responses must be recorded and analyzed according to some specified frame of reference, and the interpretation of the data must affect the future use of the materials.

Observation.   This technique involves viewing and interpreting students' behavior while they are engaged in using the instructional material. Observation differs from analytic teaching in that it is more informal. The remediation specialist merely notes students' behaviors as they occur, and then at a later time interprets what these behaviors mean in terms of modifying the instructional material.

Interviews.   This technique involves discussing with students their perceptions of the material they are using. The remediation specialist can determine whether the students find the material helpful and are motivated to use it.

10

Subject Area Tutoring

While remediation is designed to help learning disabled students acquire the skills necessary to handle college level courses, tutoring is designed to help these students to succeed in their courses. Tutoring helps students understand and master the content of their subject area courses. Learning disabilities college programs provide tutoring assistance to their students in any course in which they are enrolled. The only prerequisite for obtaining tutoring assistance is a demonstrated need on the part of the learning disabled student. According to the program directors, the most common courses for which tutoring is requested are in the areas of English, mathematics, physical sciences, and the social sciences.

PROVIDING TUTORING SERVICES

There are a number of important steps in the process of establishing an effective tutoring program for learning disabled students. Since there are differences in the tutoring services provided by the various college learning disabilities programs we visited, we cannot present a precise model. The reader will need to pick and choose ideas from the following presentation to develop a tutoring program consistent with the professional's philosophy and suitable for the institution where the program will be housed.

Selecting Tutors

Tutors can be obtained from two major sources. The first is students who are enrolled in learning disability teacher-training programs or subject area majors within the college or university. We refer to these as peer tutors. The second is college graduates with subject area majors and/or background in learning disabilities. We refer to the second group as professional tutors.

Peer Tutors

According to the program directors, an ideal peer tutor is knowledgeable in a subject area and is enrolled in a learning disabilities teacher-training program. Vogel observed on June 15, 1982, that because these tutors are knowledgeable about both a subject area and learning disabilities, they bring a double set of skills to the tutoring effort. Vogel also noted that tutors with these double skills are difficult to find.

Peer tutors are frequently used to reduce the cost of providing tutoring services to learning disabled students. Sometimes the peer tutors are volunteers and at other times are nominally paid for the tutoring services they provide. Volunteers often provide their services as part of the requirements for a course in learning disabilities. Paid tutors are often work study students who receive the minimum wage for providing tutoring services.

There are some potential problems when using students as a source of tutors. These problems unfortunately most often manifest themselves at the worst possible time of the semester for learning disabled students, during the time when the learning disabled student has to prepare for examinations. Peer tutors often have competing responsibilities during examination time and are often unable to give learning disabled students the time and assistance required, since the peer tutors have to prepare for their own examinations. Another major problem is tutoring continuity. Peer tutors change from semester-to-semester and year-to-year and oftentimes have legitimate reasons for being off campus for activities that interfere with the continuity of tutoring.

Student tutors should meet a number of standards. They should be either enrolled in or have completed the same course as the student who needs the tutoring; have excelled in the course in which they are tutoring as demonstrated by a B or higher final grade in the course or in the case of a student taking the course concurrently with the tutee, a B or higher average in similar courses; have an overall 3.0 or higher grade point average; be recommended by the professor teaching the course; have junior or senior standing in the college or university; serve as good academic and personality role models for learning disabled students; be willing to participate in a tutor's training program, maintain records, and implement the suggestions provided by supervisors; and be committed to providing tutoring throughout the semester and during examination times.

Professional Tutors

The two major sources of professional tutors are subject area teachers and learning disabilities teachers. The ideal professional tutor has a subject area specialty and is familiar with learning disabilities. This combination is difficult to find among professional tutors.

Five good sources of professional tutors are:

1. Faculty spouses, many of whom have master's degrees or advanced training in subject area specialties and welcome the opportunity to use some of their free time to tutor learning disabled college students.
2. Teachers, on leave to raise families, who have small blocks of time available and want to be active in their profession.
3. Retired teachers who want to stay partially active in their profession.
4. Fulltime teachers who tutor after school hours to supplement their incomes.
5. Fulltime tutors who make a living by providing tutoring services.

While professional tutors are more expensive than peer tutors, they provide considerably more tutoring continuity. They bring a higher level of training to bear upon the problems of learning disabled college students. They frequently have very flexible schedules, so they can tutor the learning disabled college students during the daytime rather than at night. Professional tutors do not have competing responsibilities to meet course requirements of their own as do peer tutors. They are generally mature individuals who have a stabilizing effect upon learning disabled students. Professional tutors should meet a number of standards. They should have a college major or minor in the areas in which they are tutoring; have some successful experience working with high school students or young adults; have a working knowledge of learning disabilities or be willing to participate in a training program designed to build such an awareness; have a flexible schedule so tutoring sessions can be arranged at times when students are not in classes; be willing to tutor more than one day a week to accommodate learning disabled students who frequently need to be tutored two or three times per week in each subject area; and demonstrate a willingness to work cooperatively with the learning disability program supervisor and course instructors.

Training Tutors

College learning disabilities programs should have a formal tutor-training component. At the beginning of the year, approximately two or three days will be needed to acquaint the tutors with the tutoring program management plan and specific tutoring techniques. Once the program is underway, the program director or assistant director should meet with the tutoring staff on a weekly basis to focus upon specific problems encountered by the tutors.

The goals of a tutor-training program should be to teach tutors to do the following.

1. Understand the special needs of learning disabled college students as they attempt to handle their subject area course assignments
2. Help learning disabled students become independent learners
3. Provide success experiences so learning disabled students are not discouraged from learning subject matter material
4. Help learning disabled students understand the requirements and objectives of the courses in which they are enrolled
5. Prepare structured lessons with each unit divided into small parts
6. Relate their tutoring to real life experiences
7. Help the students understand and recall subject matter information, and help students develop ways to commit facts and information to memory
8. Help learning disabled college students establish study goals and specific objectives
9. Help learning disabled students prioritize and schedule their assignments
10. Help learning disabled students organize their study areas
11. Conduct study sessions
12. Use the management system of the learning disabilities college program

Assigning Tutors

The relationship between a tutor and the tutee is a very critical one. The tutor serves as both a teacher and a counselor. In many cases, a special relationship is developed that enables the tutor to push the tutee to heights in achievement that would not otherwise be attainable.

Nash pointed out on June 17, 1982, that when the personalities of the tutor and the tutee mesh, something good occurs for both. When the personalities do not mesh, the desired student achievement is not attained no matter how much knowledge or skills the tutor has. Cordoni (1980) also recognized the importance of personality factors in the tutor-tutee relationship. She found that having tutors attend group counseling sessions with learning disabled college students improved the interpersonal relationships between tutors and tutees.

Care should be taken in matching tutors to tutees. Both tutors and tutees should be asked to identify the characteristics of the persons with whom they would like to work. An informal social gathering can be used to help tutors and tutees identify specific persons with whom they want to work. Final pairing of tutors and tutees should be completed by the program staff member responsible for coordinating tutoring services using this information. Trial periods should be arranged and specified dates identified when tutors or tutees might be changed.

Scheduling Tutoring Sessions

The number of weekly tutoring sessions for a specific course should be based upon the students' prior knowledge of the subject, levels of basic skills achievement, and the difficulty level of the course. We believe the number of tutoring sessions scheduled for students should be a function of these three variables.

Tutoring should take place on the same day, but after the class meets. In this way, the tutor can clarify any misconceptions and immediately reinforce what was learned that day in class. A plan can also be made for completing assignments and getting ready for the next class meeting.

Tutoring may take place in the facility used by the learning disabilities program, the tutor's home, or the tutee's room. It is best to provide the tutoring at the facility used by the learning disabilities program or the tutor's home. This arrangement provides the maximum amount of structure and demonstrates to students the importance of structure for learning.

In a communication on June 9, 1982, Chandler gave particular emphasis to the importance of structure. She believes that the student should go to the same tutor, at the same place, and sit at the same table, in the same chair, and look in the same direction. She believes that tutors should teach the tutees to set up a special corner of their room just for study. Tutees should be taught not to eat or watch television in that area. The area should be reserved solely for study. Chandler believes that any activity other than study associated with a study area becomes a source of distraction.

Structuring Tutoring Sessions

The format of each tutoring session should be consistent so that learning disabled students internalize the procedure. In this way a minimal amount of time is wasted in start-up, transition, and ending activities. The following guidelines will help structure tutoring sessions.

Review assignments given by the professor during the last class session. Be sure the student understands the assignment, knows how to do it, and knows when it is due. Prepare a timeline for completing each assignment. Within the timeline, indicate the activities that are to be completed by a certain time or date.

Review information provided by the professor during the last class session. Clarify any concepts and define any words the student does not know. Keep the explanations concrete and relate them to the student's life experiences whenever possible.

Check assignments the student is about to turn in to course professors. Examine them to be sure they are consistent with the assignment made by the professor. Further, check for clarity, organization, spelling and grammar errors, and general legibility and neatness.

Assist the student to develop a plan for continued self-study. This is necessary if the student is to achieve independence. If the plan for self-study is not developed, the student will become overly dependent upon the tutor and study only when in the presence of the tutor.

Complete necessary record forms provided by the learning disabilities program. These will provide a record of each tutoring session and be helpful to supervisors who are assigned to provide guidance and suggestions to tutors.

Record Keeping Forms

Every tutor should maintain a schedule of tutoring sessions such as Table 10-1, which shows the tutoring assignments for a tutor during a specified semester or term of an academic year. In this example, the tutor has three students scheduled over five tutoring days of a week. The schedule indicates the time, number of tutoring sessions, name of tutee, subject area being tutored, and where the tutoring takes place. A copy of the Tutoring Schedule should be maintained by the tutor and a second copy given to the appropriate supervisor from the learning disabilities program.

Tutors must also maintain a daily log of tutoring activities. These logs should be kept in separate folders for each tutee. Table 10-2 shows a sample tutoring log. The tutoring log has a place to indicate the name of the student, the title of the course for which the student is being tutored, the tutor's name, the date of the tutoring session, the time the student arrives for the session, and the time the student left. Sufficient space is provided

Table 10-1 Tutoring Schedule Form

Tutoring Schedule for *(name of tutor)*

Semester ———, 19 ———

Time	Monday	Tuesday	Wednesday	Thursday	Friday
9–10 AM	Marie (Biology) Room 123	———	Marie (Biology) Room 123	———	Marie (Biology) Room 123
11–12 noon	———	Max (History) Room 127	———	Max (History) Room 127	
1–2 PM	Jake (Physiology) Room 131	———	Jake (Physiology) Room 131	———	
2–3 PM	———	Jake (Physiology) Room 123	———	Jake (Physiology) Room 123	

Table 10-2 Tutoring Log Form

Tutoring Log

Student _____ Course _____ Tutor _____

Date _____ Time In _____ Time Out _____

Assignments reviewed:

Information explained:

Assignments checked:

Study plan:

Comments:

---

for a brief comment about each guideline for structuring tutoring sessions we previously discussed. Space is also available for comments the tutor wishes to communicate to a supervisor.

The tutoring log should be reviewed each week by a learning disabilities program supervisor. Tutors should provide sufficient information so a supervisor can use the information to provide them with guidance or teaching suggestions.

Table 10-3 shows a sample form that can be used by tutors to evaluate tutees. This or a similar form should be completed weekly by tutors and forwarded to the appropriate learning disabilities program supervisor. The information obtained from this form may suggest the need for counseling, increasing or decreasing tutoring, changes in the remediation plan, or adjustments in other services that can be provided through the learning disabilities program. This form for evaluating tutees is limited to six items that assess the important variables related to tutoring effectiveness.

Table 10-4 provides a sample form that can be used by tutees to evaluate their tutors. This form should be completed once a week by the tutees and given to the appropriate supervisor from the learning disabilities program. This form for evaluating tutors is limited to six items that assess the important variables that relate to tutoring effectiveness. The information obtained from this form may suggest the need for changing tutors or providing the tutor with suggestions for improving the tutor's effectiveness.

Table 10-3 Evaluation of Tutee Form

Tutor Evaluation of Tutee

Tutee _____ Course _____
Week _____ Tutor _____

Directions: Read each sentence and the words that follow it. Circle the word(s) that
tell how you feel about the sentence. Comment freely.

1. My tutee arrives for appointments on time.
    Strongly agree   Agree   Disagree   Strongly disagree
    Comment:

2. My tutee brings assignments and materials.
    Strongly agree   Agree   Disagree   Strongly disagree
    Comment:

3. My tutee stays on-task for the entire tutoring session.
    Strongly agree   Agree   Disagree   Strongly disagree
    Comment:

4. My tutee follows the study plan for continued self-study.
    Strongly agree   Agree   Disagree   Strongly disagree
    Comment:

5. My tutee is achieving satisfactorily.
    Strongly agree   Agree   Disagree   Strongly disagree
    Comment:

6. My tutee is becoming a more independent learner.
    Strongly agree   Agree   Disagree   Strongly disagree
    Comment:

Is there anything special you want to say about your tutee? Write it here.

Table 10-4 Evaluation of Tutor Form

Tutee Evaluation of Tutor

Tutor _____   Course _____
Week_____   Tutee _____

Directions: Read each sentence and the words that follow it. Circle the word(s) that
tell how you feel about the sentence. Comment freely.

1. My tutor begins and ends each session on time.
    Strongly agree   Agree   Don't know   Disagree   Strongly disagree

2. My tutor helps me understand my assignments.
    Strongly agree   Agree   Don't know   Disagree   Strongly disagree

3. My tutor helps me understand the professor and course materials.
    Strongly agree   Agree   Don't know   Disagree   Strongly disagree

4. My tutor checks my assignments before I turn them in to the professor.
    Strongly agree   Agree   Don't know   Disagree   Strongly disagree

5. My tutor helps me make a plan for studying the course material on my own.
    Strongly agree   Agree   Don't know   Disagree   Strongly disagree

6. I am doing better in my course because of my tutor.
    Strongly agree   Agree   Don't know   Disagree   Strongly disagree

Is there anything special you want to say about your tutor? Write it here.

_____

Contact With Professors

Prior to the first tutoring session, the tutor should meet with the
course professor. The tutor should request a course syllabus and any
appropriate handouts. Both the syllabus and handouts should be reviewed
and the professor asked to indicate those topics for which tutoring would
be most helpful for the student. The tutor and professor should exchange
phone numbers and agree upon specific dates when they will contact each
other to share information about the student's progress and needs.

Professors should be assured that their responsibilities are very
minimal as far as tutoring is concerned. Basically, all a professor has to do is
be cooperative and be willing to share information about the student's
progress in the course. It should be made clear to the professor that there is
no need to lower standards for the learning disabled student.

Contact between professors and tutors is critical to the success of a tutoring program. This is particularly so at the beginning of the year when the tutee is likely to bring more misinformation than correct information to the tutoring sessions. Tutoring that is specific to a professor's perceived needs for a tutee is likely to enhance the professor's perception of the learning disability program, the tutor, and the tutee.

Materials

The course syllabus, textbook, handouts, reading lists, and assignment sheets are the main materials necessary to provide focus for the tutoring sessions. It would also be helpful to have available supplementary textbooks that might explain concepts in a simpler manner, as well as reference books such as a dictionary and a thesaurus. Sometimes it is necessary to provide specialized materials for a subject. For geography, for example, the tutor should have an atlas available. The principle to keep in mind is that tutoring should take place with the actual materials used by the professor teaching the course supplemented by materials that help the tutor explain concepts in a simpler fashion.

11

Special Courses

Special courses are frequently offered for students enrolled in learning disabilities college programs. The purpose of these courses is to provide students with the necessary prerequisite skills and social and emotional awareness to succeed in college. These special courses are usually required and offered for groups of learning disabled students. These courses may be taught by staff members from the learning disabilities program or by faculty members from academic departments. In some cases two instructors, one from the program and one from the academic department, teach the course using a team teaching approach. In some cases, academic departments offer special sections of their regular courses for learning disabled students.

Special courses offered by the college learning disabilities program typically focus on nonacademic aspects of college students' learning disabilities such as study skills and college survival. These help students adjust to the academic demands of college and are usually noncredit courses. When courses were offered through academic departments, they were for credit and focused upon subject area content at an introductory level. While the objectives of courses offered through academic departments were not altered for the learning disabled students, the teaching styles were adjusted for the learning disabilities of the students. For example, professors tended to reduce the time they spent lecturing in favor of the use of visual aids such as films and extensive use of the chalkboard.

Many special courses were offered to learning disabled students through the programs we examined. There was no standard set of courses offered to learning disabled students. The courses offered often reflected identified needs of the learning disabled college students enrolled in a program at a specific college or university. The following statements identify and describe special courses offered to learning disabled students at the various colleges and universities we examined. Staff of learning disabilities college programs should consider offering these courses subject to their analysis of the needs of students in their own programs.

EXAMPLES OF SPECIAL COURSES

College Survival

Martin, on June 29, 1982, described a one-credit, student development course offered to all entering learning disabled students at Montgomery College. This special course is established to help learning disabled students acquire the information and learn about the resources necessary to "survive" in the college mainstream through their own efforts. Through the course, the students acquire study habits and learn how to compensate for their individual learning difficulties.

Basic Reading and Writing Courses

Martin also described a basic reading and two basic writing courses offered at Montgomery College for learning disabled students. Basic Reading, Basic Writing I, and Basic Writing II are designed to help students acquire the necessary skills for entrance into regular college level English courses. In these noncredit courses, the students receive small group and individualized instruction concentrating on oral expression, listening skills, grammar, paragraph development, word attack skills, vocabulary development, and reading comprehension.

Developmental Reading and English Composition

Rosenthal, Fine, and deVight (1982) described a series of combined developmental reading and English composition courses taught at Kingsborough Community College. Students who score below the minimum cutoff level of the college placement examination are required to take one or more of these courses. These noncredit courses integrate reading and English instruction rather than assigning each to its own separate course.

English Composition

Cordoni reported on June 21, 1982, that at Southern Illinois University, learning disabled students were able to enroll in a special section of English Composition 101 offered through the English department. The requirements are the same as for other sections of the course; however, this special section is team taught by a faculty member from the learning disability program and a faculty member from the English Department. While the special section of English 101 covers the same content as all other sections, it does so in a manner more compatible with the way learning disabled college students learn. The students receive English credit for this course.

Fundamentals of Communication

Saddler explained (July 14, 1982) that at the College of the Ozarks, learning disabled students are able to take a course titled Fundamentals of Communication. This course is a precursor to freshman composition and is designed to raise students' skills to the entry level for freshman composition. Students who take the course do so on a pass/fail basis and do not receive credit for the course toward their degree completion.

Language Remediation

Nash, in a communication on June 17, 1982, reported that all students participating in Project Success at the University of Wisconsin, Oshkosh, had to complete a language remediation course. Procedures employed by the course instructors are designed to teach students the phonetic nature of American English to assist them to decode-read and encode-spell American English words.

Typing

On June 17, 1982, Vernoy recommended a typing course to many of his students in his program at Wright State University. Vernoy, however, does not recommend the regular university typing courses because they have a heavy grammar emphasis that is too difficult for the learning disabled students. Vernoy prefers to have his students taught basic typing without the heavy emphasis upon grammar. He recommends that learning disabled college students take a typing course through the evening division at a high school. To avoid inconveniencing students, we recommend that staff of learning disabilities programs develop their own typing courses or work with the department offering typing to develop special sections. Staff members may wish to use the *Typing Keys for the Remediation of Reading and Spelling Difficulties* which we describe in the next chapter of this book.

Personal Psychology

Webb reported on July 15, 1982, that students in the Program of Assistance in Learning (PAL) are required to take a three-week minicourse

Sudah di uace -le
page ini
sebelah table

in personal psychology. This course is offered during the summer prior to the students' first semester of classes at Curry College. The purpose of the course is to help students understand their learning strengths and weaknesses and to recognize their learning style.

Study Skills

Barbara (1982) described a study skills course offered at Adelphi University to learning disabled students who were admitted to a five-week diagnostic session held during the summer prior to their first semester on campus. The course is used to assess students' readiness for college level work and is the only required special course learning disabled students have to take at Adelphi University. Results from this course provide part of the data that staff use to determine if students are ready to be admitted to the fall academic program. The study skills course focuses upon a number of important aspects. Learning disabled students are taught to read college level textbooks effectively and efficiently, use Recordings for the Blind, develop strategies for remembering important information, listen to lectures with more understanding, expand their vocabulary, prepare for and take course examinations, read with better understanding, write more effectively, prepare research papers, and make good use of the library. Students do not receive credit for taking this course, which is taught by Adelphi University students holding at least a master's degree in special education.

MULTIPLE OFFERINGS OF SPECIAL COURSES

Some programs for learning disabled students offer a number of special courses for their students. The results from diagnostic tests are used to determine which of the courses will be required for each student. A sample of the array of courses offered by some college programs is provided here.

Bookman and Dyer reported on October 25, 1982, that learning disabled students at Metropolitan State College are provided with alternative methods of instruction in one or more areas based upon their diagnostic profiles. The materials used in the courses were developed by the professional staff, and the courses are taught by upper division college work study students, teachers working toward recertification, and graduate students. Some courses are taught on a one-to-one basis and others in small groups. The courses are offered for credit. The program offers special courses in: Phonics Strategies, Spelling Strategies, Reading Strategies, Math Concepts, Vocabulary and Word Usage, Content Reading Improvement, and Language Structure and Grammatical Analysis.

On April 22, 1982, Dillon reported that at Moorpark College learning disabled students may enroll in a variety of learning skills classes. These small group classes provide instruction at the appropriate levels in reading, spelling, writing, and mathematics. A class in personal growth and development is also available.

Vogel reported on June 16, 1982, that at Barat College, learning disabled students may take special courses in writing, reading, mathematics, effective study habits, life/career planning, assertiveness training, and interpersonal communication skills. These courses are offered for college credits that apply toward graduation.

Barsch reported, in a communication in July 1982, that at Ventura College, 15 courses are offered through the learning skills center. Each course is offered for 3 credit hours. Special courses include: mathematics, reading, spelling, memory power, learning to listen, vocabulary building, personal discovery, study skills, perceptual-motor training, creative thinking and problem solving, assessment of learning skills, and others as the need for them is demonstrated. Ventura is a community college providing services to over 300 learning disabled students every year. Typically, community or junior colleges offer more and a wider range of special courses than four-year colleges or universities.

Dickerson reported on February 10, 1982, that at The American University, at least 12 special courses are offered through The Learning Services, which is a support service for learning disabled students. Through this support service, students are able to work with counselors to complete many courses ranging from 1 to 30 hours in length. Special courses offered are: rapid reading (15 hours), comprehension (1 hour and up), notetaking (1 hour and up), vocabulary building (1 hour and up), grammar and structure (2 hours and up), writing organization (3 hours and up), spelling (3 hours and up), taking examinations (3 hours), personal typing (30 hours), preparing the finished copy (1 hour), time management (2 hours), and competency exam preparation (3 hours and up).

Saddler reported (July 14, 1982) that at the College of the Ozarks, the staff of the learning disabilities program presents in-class workshops demonstrating how basic study skills can apply to various content areas. Members of the staff also teach a course in Developmental Reading and General Study Skills, supervise laboratories for freshman composition, and each semester offer a workshop in how to write a research paper. The following special courses are also provided: Developmental Writing, Fundamentals of Communication, and Fundamentals of Mathematics.

Not every program director believes in offering special courses. On June 9, 1982, Chandler reported that no special courses of a remedial nature are offered to learning disabled students at Erskine College. At

Erskine College, the learning disabled students are mainstreamed from their first day on campus. Chandler believes that when a student arrives on campus, it is too late for remediation. She believes, instead, that through tutoring, her tutors can "stuff" the tutees with the information they need to succeed in their courses. As they do this, the tutors teach the students how to compensate for their learning disabilities.

12

Auxiliary Aids and Services

In this chapter we describe aids and services that are provided to learning disabled college students beyond those presented earlier in the book. Learning disabled students need to know how to use tape recorders in their classes, how to access to taped textbooks, the value of calculators for subjects such as math and science, and the value of typing. They need special services from note takers and advocates, and alternative tests and special housing arrangements. These auxiliary aids and services are detailed in this chapter. When added to the previously presented components, they make for a comprehensive program.

AUXILIARY AIDS

Auxiliary aids often provided by learning disabilities college programs include tape recorders, taped textbooks, calculators and typewriters.

Tape Recorders

Learning disabled college students often have difficulty taking written notes from class lectures. For these students tape recorders are valuable auxiliary aids for recording class lectures. Section 504 of the Rehabilitation Act of 1973 requires that handicapped students be allowed to use tape recorders in class if they can demonstrate the need for their use. Generally it is not necessary to evoke the formality of this law to gain permission for students to tape record classes. Some professors object to students taping their lectures because the professors may discuss material in class they wish to copyright. When professors object to the use of tape recorders, Vogel (1982) suggests that students should request permission to tape record classes by completing a form that indicates that the taped lectures are for use by the student only. This will reassure those professors who are concerned that their ability to copyright materials from their lectures will be jeopardized if students are able to record material verbatim on tape.

We present a form for permission to tape record class lectures in Table 12-1. Students should make an appointment with their professor to discuss their need to tape record class sessions and to ask the professor to sign the form. The form should be prepared in triplicate. One copy should be retained by the student, a second placed in the student's program file, and a third copy given to the professor.

Vogel (1982) recommends that students tape record lectures not as a substitute for note taking, but rather as a technique that allows them to listen to lectures in an unhurried manner and to integrate and organize information. Later, students can replay the tapes a number of times to understand complex ideas. Vogel emphasizes that by tape recording lectures, students may reduce the heavy demands on their auditory memory that occurs when they take written class notes.

A speech-time compressor will help students to listen to replayed lectures at slower speeds. A speech-time compressor is a device that allows the listener to select the listening speed of audio taped material without altering the pitch characteristics of the recording.

Cordoni (1980) has students in her learning disabilities program at Southern Illinois University bring their taped class lectures to the program center. Staff of the program teach students how to put the taped information in their own words for study purposes. Cordoni recommends

Table 12-1 Form for Permission to Tape Class Lectures

Dear Professor:

I am a student in your course *(name of course)*. I am also a participant in the program for learning disabled students. The nature of my learning disability makes it difficult for me to take written notes in class.

I request permission to use a tape recorder to record your class sessions. The tape recordings are for my use only. I will not share the tape recordings with anyone.

I hope you will allow me to tape record your course.

(name of student)

I give *(name of student)* permission to tape record class sessions in my course *(name of course)*.

(name of professor)
(date)

that students be taught how to transcribe notes from their tape recorded lectures. Students who cannot type need to be taught this skill.

Some staff members of learning disabilities college programs are concerned about the amount of time it takes students to listen to taped lectures. The amount of extra time that students spend listening can be reduced in two ways. One way is through the use of a steno mask. Vernoy told us on June 17, 1982, that some students in the learning disabilities college program at Wright State University used a steno mask with success. The steno mask is essentially a microphone within a mask that enables a student to talk into a tape recorder without being heard. This allows students to selectively dictate the important points as they listen to a lecture. The process is analagous to taking written notes, without the requirement of written language ability. Because only portions of the lecture are dictated, the amount of time needed to replay and listen to the lectures is reduced. A second timesaver is the use of the speech-time compressor, which was previously described. This device may be used to play tapes back at a faster than normal speed.

Students should also be encouraged to use tape recorders to rehearse information and to study for tests. By using earphones, students can review taped material at the cafeteria, the library, and even as they fall asleep at night. We recommend the use of small personal cassette players for this purpose.

Taped Textbooks

It is important to provide taped textbooks for those learning disabled students who have difficulty reading college level materials. College learning disabilities program staff members must assist these students to obtain taped textbooks. Taped textbooks, as well as other recorded books and materials, should be maintained in an audio library. Students should be allowed to check out materials from the audio library much as they would from a standard library.

There are two major sources of recorded books. The primary resource for college learning disabilities programs is: Recording for the Blind, Inc. (RFB), 215 E. 58th Street, New York, NY   10022; (212)   751-0860. RFB is a national nonprofit, voluntary organization that provides recorded, educational books free-on-loan to individuals who cannot read printed materials because of visual, physical, or perceptual handicaps. Persons diagnosed as dyslexic or otherwise learning disabled as a result of an organic dysfunction of sufficient severity to prevent their reading printed material in a normal manner are eligible for this service. A disability statement that appears on the application form must be signed by either a medical specialist or by a learning disabilities specialist.

RFB has a Master Tape Library containing over 55,000 textbook titles.

New books are recorded at the rate of approximately 4000 per year. Copies of any of the recorded titles from the Master Tape Library are duplicated and sent to registered borrowers free upon request. Recordings are loaned for a period of up to one year, and borrowers can get an extension upon written request. All book requests must be submitted in the name of the individual borrower and made in writing or by telephone.

RFB's peak request periods for student services are January–February, June–July, and August–September. Borrowers are urged to get their book requests to RFB well ahead of these months. College learning disabilities program staff should assist students in placing their textbook requests so textbooks are received in time for the beginning of the term. Textbooks should be ordered as soon as learning disabled students have registered for courses. Learning disabled students should be registered for courses far in advance of the normal registration date. This is to allow sufficient time for RFB to record textbooks and get the recordings to the students. It is important to have professors identify the texts they plan to use in their courses in advance of usual deadlines.

Upon specific request, RFB will record books not in its Master Tape Library. To have a book recorded the borrower must send two copies of the book to RFB. The books may be mailed Free Matter for the Blind, but in the interest of time it is recommended they be sent First Class, or United States Parcel Post. RFB acknowledges receipt of the books and advises the requestor on the projected dates for mailing the first and last installments. As the book is being recorded, installments are mailed directly from the recording studio to the borrower. It generally takes at least four weeks before the first installment is mailed.

RFB recorded books are provided on special format 15/16 inches per second (ips), 4-track cassettes, each containing four hours of recorded text. The RFB cassettes cannot be played on standard 2-track cassette machines. While RFB does not provide the special equipment needed to play these cassettes, compatible equipment may be purchased from the American Printing House for the Blind, 1839 Frankfurt Avenue, Louisville, KY 40206; (502) 895-2405. The American Printing House sells a portable cassette recorder/player that has two-speed operation (standard cassette speed of 1⅞ ips, and the 15/16 ips speed), and 4-track operation (plays 4-track cassette tapes or standard 2-track cassette tapes). Tapes may be recorded in 2- or 4-track format at standard speed or at the 15/16 ips speed. The current cost of the unit is $155. The purchaser must complete a form certifying that the special recorder is being purchased solely for the education or enjoyment of visually, physically, or other print handicapped readers who are unable to read regular print material.

A second major source of recorded books is the National Library Service for the Blind and Physically Handicapped (NLS), the Library of Congress, 1291 Taylor Street NW, Washington, DC   20542; (202) 287-5100.

NLS selects and produces full-length books and magazines on recorded discs and cassettes. These are distributed through a cooperating network of 56 regional and more than 100 subregional (local) libraries, where they are circulated free of charge to eligible borrowers. Individuals with a reading or learning disability are eligible if there is an organic dysfunction or physical cause of the disability, and the disability is of sufficient severity to prevent reading printed material in a normal manner. An application for services by a learning disabled individual will be approved only if there is an accompanying certification on the application form by a medical doctor or doctor of osteopathy indicating that the disability results from organic dysfunction. These medical specialists may consult with colleagues in associated disciplines such as a school psychologist or learning disabilities teacher.

Eligible readers may borrow all types of popular-interest books including best sellers, classics, mysteries, westerns, poetry, history, biographies, religious literature, children's books, and foreign-language materials. Readers may also subscribe to more than 70 popular magazines.

NLS records books (often referred to as "Talking Books") in two formats. One format is on discs, which may be played on a talking-book phonograph. The second format is on cassettes, which are recorded at 15/16 ips requiring the special cassette player described for RFB. Both types of special equipment are supplied to eligible persons on an extended loan basis. In addition to being used to play Talking Books borrowed from NLS, the special cassette player may be used to play recorded textbooks received from RFB. The reading material and equipment supplied by NLS may be used in public or private schools where handicapped students are enrolled. The students in these schools, however, must be certified as eligible on an individual basis and must be the direct and only recipients of the material and equipment.

Currently NLS maintains a national book collection of more than 38,000 titles. An up-to-date directory of regional and subregional libraries may be obtained by writing to NLS. Participants in the reading program receive a free subscription to *Talking Books Topics*, which is published bimonthly. This publication covers news of developments and activities in library services, and lists recorded books and magazines available through the national network of cooperating libraries. Many additional informative publications are available free from NLS.

The role of the staff of college learning disabilities programs regarding taped books is primarily a facilitative one. The staff members familiarize students with the RFB and NLS services and assist the students to complete the necessary application forms. They also help the students to identify the textbooks they will need in their courses, complete the forms, and mail them properly. We suggest that students give their return addresses as the learning disabilities program office. In this way staff of the program can keep records of books received and notify students when they are available. The recorded books should be kept in an audio library maintained by program staff. Students can check the books out on an as-needed basis. This arrangement allows the maximum number of students to benefit from the RFB and NLS services.

It is important for learning disabilities programs to include some means of recording materials through their own resources to supplement the services of RFB and NLS. This is necessary when professors assign textbooks too late for recording through these services, when important class handouts need to be recorded, and when outside reading requirements are made as courses progress. Volunteers should be recruited to tape record this material as needed. The volunteers should have good speaking voices, clear enunciation, and some familiarity with the subject matter. In some emergency cases, volunteers may need to read material directly to learning disabled students.

Some learning disabled students have difficulty using taped textbooks, and others do not like to use them. To make taped textbooks more desirable and easier to use for these students, we recommend the staff of learning disabilities programs use the procedures identified by Deshler and Graham (1980). Deshler and Graham sugested that in place of verbatim tapes, learning disabilities specialists could record a special version of the text in which they do the following.

1. With assistance from subject matter experts, identify the critical content of the text related to the course objectives, and record only those sections of the text
2. Build into their recording study skills such as previewing techniques and study questions
3. Highlight important points
4. Intersperse paraphrased paragraphs with verbatim reading
5. Explain abstract terms
6. Repeat key concepts

The recommendations proposed by Deshler and Graham (1980), when followed, make available to learning disabled students tape recordings with a very specialized format and cue system. As a general principle students should read along in their textbooks whenever listening to the tape recording. This should be done for verbatim recordings or selected recordings. When using a special system such as that of Deshler and Graham (1980), the specialist preparing the audio tape must mark the textbook in a manner that allows the student to follow the text. Deshler and Graham (1980) propose a visual marking system in which a wavy line is made in the left-hand margin for material that is paraphrased, a dotted line for material that is deleted, and a solid line for material that is read verbatim.

Because not all learning disabled students are helped by the use of taped textbooks, but most think they would be, Vogel (1982) emphasizes the importance of periodically evaluating the progress of students using this device. She maintains that only those students who have benefited from using taped materials should be encouraged to continue to use them. She further emphasizes the importance of teaching learning disabled students the effective use of taped materials and ways of enhancing their comprehension and retention of information contained in taped material.

Calculators

Some learning disabled college students understand mathematic concepts, but have not mastered computational skills to a level of automatic accuracy. These students find the use of calculators helpful for solving mathematic problems. Calculators that contain basic mathematic functions should be provided to these students through the resources of the learning disabilities program. Staff members with mathematic background should teach the students to use the calculators efficiently and effectively. Permission should be obtained for students to use calculators in their mathematics courses and perhaps when taking tests.

Typewriters

Many learning disabled students have underdeveloped handwriting skills. Written assignments can become tests of endurance for these students rather than measures of their grasp of information. These students should be taught to use electric typewriters, preferably machines with some memory. Frequently students' spelling ability is improved when they use a typewriter with memory ability. The memory function allows students to proofread and immediately correct errors with ease.

Cordoni (1979b) recommends the use of *Typing Keys for the Remediation of Reading and Spelling Difficulties,* published by Academic Therapy Publications, 20 Commercial Boulevard, Novato, CA   94947. This program decreases the amount of visual stimulation normally present in a typing course, while incorporating the auditory and haptic channels in the teaching of this skill.

AUXILIARY SERVICES

Auxiliary services provided by learning disabilities college programs include notetakers, alternative test arrangements, advocacy, and special housing arrangements.

Notetakers

In most colleges learning disabilities programs, notetakers are provided for the students. This is an alternative to tape recording class lectures when professors are reluctant to be tape recorded.

Most often notetakers are non–learning-disabled students who are attending classes with the learning disabled student. They are students who have been identified as good notetakers by the learning disabled students, professors, or staff members of the learning disabilities college programs. Notetakers must be reliable, competent in the subject, and have legible handwriting.

In some programs notetakers are paid. Chandler (communication, June 9, 1982), paid notetakers a small amount of money when they assisted learning disabled students in her program at Erskine College. She found paying notetakers a minimal fee encouraged them to be active and careful notetakers. The notetakers at Erskine College did not know for whom they were taking notes. They left duplicate notes with Chandler, who then distributed the notes to the learning disabled students. In this way, the learning disabled students were able to remain anonymous.

In other programs notetakers were not paid. In these cases notetakers were usually given paper to use for taking duplicate notes. Where programs did not provide notetakers, learning disabled students were encouraged to ask fellow students for copies of their notes. Vernoy recommended, on June 17, 1982, that learning disabled students offer to pay for all paper used by fellow students who agreed to share notes.

We recommend that notetakers be furnished a copy of the National Technical Institute for the Deaf (NTID) Notetaking System. This system consists of a binder for storing 8½ by 11 treated paper that is used for making copies of notes. The cost of the binder is $2.75, and paper is available in packs of 200 sheets at a cost of $4.95 per pack. Quantity discounts are available. These materials may be ordered from: The Rochester Institute of Technology Book Store, One Lomb Memorial Drive, Rochester, NY 14623; (716) 475-2504.

We believe that when notetakers are provided or when lectures are taped, learning disabled students must still attend class and take written notes. The very act of taking notes forces the student to pay attention and be an active participant in the class sessions. Students can also learn how they are developing the skill of taking notes by comparing their notes with those of the notetakers and other students in the class.

Alternative Testing Arrangements

When necessary, the staff of learning disabilities college programs make arrangements for their students to take tests in alternative ways. Alternative testing arrangements are necessary for those students who have difficulty taking conventional course examinations because of significant reading deficiencies, writing deficiencies, and/or excessive anxiety.

Here are some of the alternatives to conventional testing made available to learning disabled students. Students take the same test but with extended time limits. This helps learning disabled students who find it difficult to complete tests within the time normally provided. For students who have difficulty reading, questions are often dictated by the professors onto an audio tape. The students can then listen to and understand the questions without the interference of their reading problem. A variation of the preceding alternative is to have a proctor read the questions to the students. This allows the proctor to make sure that the students understand the questions. Sometimes students would read the examination questions but dictate their answers to the proctors. For students who have writing problems, this is very important when they have to answer essay questions. A variation on the preceding alternative is to have students dictate their answers on audio cassette tapes. Students with writing difficulties who know how to type are allowed to type their answers to questions. This reduces writing fatigue and allows students to develop their answers completely. Students may be allowed to complete their examinations at home or complete special projects in place of class examinations. Students are permitted to take a different format of an examination. For example, if they have difficulty writing, they may be allowed to take a multiple choice examination in place of an essay examination.

Once a professor agreed to permit a learning disabled student to take a test in an alternative manner, all the professor had to do was send a copy of the test to the program office. The program staff made all arrangements for the actual testing and returned the completed test to the professor.

It was not unusual for professors to initially resist the idea of having students take tests in alternative ways. Their major concern was that this would give the learning disabled student an unfair advantage over other students in the class. Program staff members assured professors that this would not be the case. They emphasized that alternative testing arrangements would serve only to ensure that the professor's test measured the student's mastery of course objectives rather than reflected the student's learning disability. Cordoni reported on June 21, 1982, that when she experienced resistance, she volunteered to go personally to a professor's department and give the student the alternative form of the test there. She rarely had to do this.

Saddler (communication, July 14, 1982) told professors that when proctors wrote responses to test questions, it was the students' responses that they were writing. His proctors routinely corrected students' language as they wrote responses. When a professor objected, responses were written exactly as given by the student. Saddler told us that after the professors received an examination written in this way, they ceased objecting to the rewriting.

Hartman and Redden (1982) developed an informative guide for testing and evaluating the progress of students with disabilities. While their guide is not specifically addressed to the needs of learning disabled students, the suggestions they raised and the issues they discussed have considerable relevance when developing testing arrangements for learning disabled students.

Advocacy

In learning disabilities college programs, students are encouraged to act as their own advocates. Those students with the interpersonal skills and willingness to speak to professors about their own problems are encouraged to do so. These students are seen by program staff as approaching independence and self-sufficiency, which are two important goals of the learning disabilities college program.

Program staff members served as advocates for students when the students lacked the interpersonal skills, were unwilling or not ready to speak for themselves, or when they had unusual difficulties with their instructors. The advocate phoned the professor for an appointment and accompanied the student to the professor's office where the problems were discussed. Cordoni (communication, June 21, 1982) provided a range of options to her learning disabled students. She allowed her students to: go to the instructor on their own, take a staff member along, or request that a staff member go instead of them. Nash (communication, June 17, 1982) used a modeling technique to demonstrate to his learning disabled students how to interact with their professors. The students were able to observe staff members discuss and resolve problems with professors until they were ready to assume the role of being their own advocates.

Some college students did not want their professors to know they were learning disabled. For these students the advocacy function by program staff was suspended. Leonard (communication, June 23, 1982) found that students with mild learning disabilities preferred to remain anonymous, while those with more severe learning disabilities wanted their professors to be aware of their difficulties.

Some of the activities performed by program staff in their advocacy role include the following.

1. Requesting lists of required textbooks for taping
2. Obtaining permission for students to tape record lectures

3. Obtaining permission to use a non-class member as a notetaker
4. Requesting opportunities for students to take tests in alternative ways
5. Arranging for incomplete grades when students needed more time to complete a course
6. Arranging for withdrawal from a course without a grade penalty when extra time was not the answer
7. Helping professors understand the needs of learning disabled students in their classes
8. Providing suggestions to professors for modifying their teaching style to enhance the learning opportunities for learning disabled students
9. Serving as a surrogate parent for the student at times of crises and emergency
10. Serving as a liaison between the student and the student's parents

Vogel (1982) reported that professors were particularly flexible and willing to cooperate when the advocate from the learning disabilities program was also a member of the teaching faculty. Advocacy was always easier to perform when the advocate was the program director or assistant director, or a senior faculty member. Sometimes program staff used department chairpersons or senior faculty members within the department to advocate with other members of the department on behalf of the students.

Special Housing Arrangements

Where learning disabled students attend college away from home, careful consideration must be given to their dormitory assignments. Program directors have varying philosophies concerning dormitory arrangements. In some programs, same-sexed learning disabled students live together in the same dormitory. Program directors who favor this arrangement believe that it promotes a sense of camaraderie and program solidarity. Other directors favor having students assigned to dormitories along with all other students at the college. These directors believe that learning disabled students must learn to accept and feel comfortable with college life in the most natural manner.

Regardless of which arrangement is used, it is important that learning disabled students have available a quiet, nondistracting environment for studying and be supervised by house parents who provide stable emotional support. Structure is also important. Learning disabled students should be required to observe curfew and abide by established rules concerning visitors, "lights out," and playing the radio, records, or tapes.

A LOOK TO THE FUTURE

Ignacio Götz, director of the Program for Academic Learning Skills (PALS) at Hofstra University, is particularly proud of the fact that students in his program work with microcomputers. PALS has two microcomputers with simple word processing programs that the students can use to write papers. Students are able to store what they write and make whatever number of revisions are necessary. Once students are satisfied with their papers, they can direct the microcomputer to print them. A word-check program is available so that the students will know whether or not they have any misspelled words in their papers.

Microcomputers hold enormous potential for learning disabled students. We recommend that program directors follow the lead of Götz and find ways that microcomputers can be used to increase their students' success in college.

13

Providing Counseling Services

Professionals working with learning disabled college students have gained increased awareness of the social and personal difficulties experienced by these individuals. College learning disabled students frequently experience difficulty forming good interpersonal relationships and accepting and responding constructively to the limitations imposed by their learning disability. To assist students with these difficulties, learning disabilities college programs provide a variety of personal counseling opportunities. These include group counseling, informal rap sessions, individual counseling, and career counseling.

Most learning disabilities college programs provide counseling for students on a voluntary basis. Some programs, such as the one at Adelphi University, require students to participate in group and individual counseling. In the Adelphi University program, staff believe that by requiring students to participate in counseling, they are able to provide help to learning disabled students who may not be aware of their need for counseling.

Learning disabilities college programs use personnel with various backgrounds to provide counseling services. In some cases counseling is done by the program director or by a learning disabilities specialist on the program staff. In other cases the programs hire counseling specialists or social workers to provide this service. Learning disabilities programs at colleges and universities that have a counseling center sometimes use its personnel to provide counseling service to the students in their program. In large colleges and universities, a counselor from the counseling center may be specifically designated to work with the learning disabled students.

Nash, in a communication on June 17, 1982, preferred to use professionals who themselves are learning disabled individuals as counselors in his program at the University of Wisconsin—Oshkosh. He believes that counselors who are themselves learning disabled can establish a close and empathic relationship with their learning disabled clients.

Staff members of learning disabilities college programs use structured and directive counseling approaches to help learning disabled students organize their behavior and focus on goals and objectives. These techniques include assertiveness training, role-playing, modeling, cognitive restructuring, self-verbalizations, and the use of visual aids (Lutwak and Fine, 1983).

COUNSELING GOALS

Counseling is an important component of learning disabilities college programs. Counseling: offers learning disabled students a sounding board for their perceptions, ideas, and feelings; and creates an opportunity for these students to explore and understand themselves and their interactions with others (Rosenthal et al., 1982).

Six goals of counseling learning disabled college students are to help the students to:

1. *Reduce anxiety.* Reducing the anxiety level of learning disabled students as they cope with college demands is a continuous activity. The slightest change in learning disabled students' situation can cause their anxiety to rise dramatically.
2. *Increase self-confidence.* Because of their history of underachievement, learning disabled students lack self-confidence. It is important to recognize their accomplishments with positive reinforcement. Learning disabled students often interpret the absence of reinforcement as negative reinforcement.
3. *Increase socialization.* Most learning disabled students are loners. They often withdraw in order to conceal their deficits. In some cases, they manipulate the behavior of others as a defense tactic. Withdrawal or manipulation both produce social alienation. The need to establish trusting, social relationships is acute for learning disabled college students.
4. *Learn life skills.* Life skills assist learning disabled students to adapt more successfully to the demands of college. Counseling efforts with learning disabled college students should focus on teaching them skills in goal setting, time management, decision-making, and stress management.
5. *Understand their learning disability.* In many cases learning disabled college students have very little understanding of their problem. A

long-term counseling goal thus should be to make students aware of the nature and effects of their learning disability.

6. *Achieve a sense of normalcy.* Learning disabled students should be encouraged to emphasize their similarities rather than differences, capabilities rather than inadequacies, and potentialities rather than substandard current performances. (Johnson & Morasky, 1980; Swan, 1982*; Vogel, personal communication, June 16, 1982).

COUNSELING PRINCIPLES

Every counselor should have principles to guide their efforts when counseling learning disabled college students. Here are some helpful principles offered by Brown (1982) for working with these students.

Provide information about the handicap. Many learning disabled students have experienced learning difficulties throughout their lives without knowing the reason why. They frequently ascribe their failures to not trying, to being weak, or even to being crazy or stupid. These self-perceptions lower the students' self-concept and inhibit their desire and efforts to improve.

Present information clearly. Use both scientific words and common phrases when helping learning disabled students to understand their handicap.

Provide positive reinforcement. Learning disabled students often find it difficult to keep up with their non–learning-disabled peers. This often results in their being criticized or teased. Positive reinforcement should be given to the students whenever possible to encourage them to keep up the difficult struggle.

Acknowledge the difficulty. Students with learning disabilities do not get much sympathy, and sometimes they need to complain. It is important not to confuse ventilation with self-pity. Brown recommends using phrases such as: "It really does take a lot of work to overcome these handicaps," "I'm impressed that you stick with it and get your studying completed," "It

---

*Swan, RJ. *A counseling model for promoting academic success of learning disabled students at the university level.* Unpublished manuscript, California State University at Long Beach, 1982.

definitely takes more time to listen to your books than to read them," and, "It must be hard to watch the other students enjoying their weekends and evenings when you have to study."

Deal with self-pity.   Self-pity is natural in everyone. Learning disabled students, however, often have excessive self-pity. To help these students overcome this have them talk of their important accomplishments and provide them with praise for the things they have done.

Talk about behavior.   Focus on the students' observable behavior rather than inferred behavior. For example, rather than say to a student, "You aren't trying very hard," Brown suggests saying, "It sounds like you aren't spending enough time studying." Or, as another example, it would be helpful to say to a student, "Your history professor has told me that you spoke to him in a loud, nasty tone of voice when you asked to tape his classes. He thought you didn't show respect for him." It would be less helpful to say, "You got angry at your history professor and that's why he didn't let you tape his classes."

Provide specific feedback.   Rather than making general statements, counselors should make statements that clearly indicate what they want students to do. For example, rather than telling a student to pay attention during a counseling session, Brown suggests saying, "When your eyes wander all over the room, I feel like you're aren't listening to me. Please look at me when I am talking to you."

Be positive.   This is another important principle offered by Johnson and Morasky (1980). It is important to assure learning disabled students that they will improve. A motivational qualification must be added, however, that improvement will occur only through hard work on their part.

Lutwak and Fine (1983) caution that counselors must guard against acting countertherapeutically because of a conscious or unconscious bias about learning disabilities. They note that a learning disability places additional demands on the already complex counseling process. Counselors with limited experience in working with learning disabled clients may feel tense, uneasy, and uncertain. In some cases a counselor may feel overwhelmed by the learning disability, becoming frustrated and anxious in their interactions with the learning disabled individual. Lutwak and Fine suggest that counselors working with learning disabled college students fully explore and resolve their feelings so they may function as instruments of positive growth and change.

FORMS OF COUNSELING

Learning disabilities college programs provide group and/or individual counseling sessions for their students. Group sessions are the typical format. Individual counseling sessions are provided when students have serious problems.

Group Counseling

Vogel observed on June 16, 1982, that group sessions provided an important sharing of information as well as mutual support for learning disabled college students. Learning disabled students are able to learn successful coping and adaptive strategies from each other. Seeing that others have the same problems helps each student accept their own disability in a constructive manner. Many suppressed anxieties and concerns surface. Vogel reported that initial group sessions were characterized by an opening-up in which participants described situations they had to face and how they attempted to deal with them. Typically, close friendships developed after a few group sessions.

Cordoni (1982b) noted that group sessions were often the first opportunity learning disabled college students had to openly talk with other learning disabled individuals about their feelings. It was obvious to her that many students needed to talk things out. The group sessions

Table 13-1 Group Counseling Session Summary

Date _____	Counselor _____
Location _____	Participants _____ _____
Time: began _____	_____ _____
ended _____	_____ _____
	_____ _____
	_____ _____

I.   *Problems Discussed* (cite names as appropriate)

II. *Reactions*

III. *Recommended Actions*

IV. *Goals for Next Session*

provided a valuable framework for open discussion and subsequent role-modeling by those students who had managed to overcome their problems.

Students had many problems in common. Examples of problems often experienced by learning disabled college students included: dealing with the side effects of medication; not knowing what to say or do in various social situations; having difficulty getting dates; resentment over having to spend more time on coursework than their non–learning-disabled peers; difficulty keeping track of course assignments; difficulty establishing close friendships; anxiety about taking tests; lack of time for fun and relaxation; feelings of being unable to do anything well; and worrying whether they would always have a learning disability.

A form for summarizing group counseling sessions is shown in Table 13-1. Using this form the counselor can record the types of problems discussed, responses to the problems, and actions to be taken by the group or specific students. The counselor can also specify the goals for the next counseling session.

Informal Rap Sessions

It is not uncommon for students in learning disabilities college programs to hold spontaneous rap sessions (also referred to in the literature as peer support groups, self-help groups, and social interaction groups). Cordoni (communication, June 21, 1982) found that students in her program at Southern Illinois University frequently got spontaneous informal rap sessions going during the course of social activities.

While less structured than formal group sessions, rap sessions have a number of advantages. They can be conducted anywhere at any time; can deal with real problems on-the-spot; allow learning disabled students opportunities for leadership; can last as long as students feel necessary; allow students to receive continual feedback from peers; allow students to monitor their personal interactions with others; allow students to advocate for and with one another; show students that learning disabled individuals can adapt to college successfully; and do not require the services of a professional counselor.

Because the learning disabled students select the topics emphasized in the rap sessions, the topics are highly relevant to the needs of the students. Ugland and Duane (1976) found frequent emphasis on the themes of assertiveness, taking responsibility, and social participation.

Individual Counseling

Individual counseling sessions are necessary when students have serious, personal problems. Sensitive topics such as difficulty with the opposite sex, or family conflicts, are best dealt with individually. A significant practical limitation of individual counseling is its relative expense. Because of the expense factor group sessions are more frequently utilized in learning disabilities college programs.

Career Counseling

The affective and learning problems of learning disabled college students often result in these students setting self-goals that are lower than their capability and potential. Blalock and Dixon (1982) cautioned that a fear of new situations, founded on a history of rejections and failures, may lead learning disabled students to opt for less threatening but potentially less satisfying career directions. This would then be reflected in students' choice of a college major. Consequently Vogel and Sattler (1981) emphasized the importance of helping learning disabled college students to select a major and determine career goals that were consistent with their abilities and deficits.

Hartman (1981) emphasized the importance of nonrestrictive career counseling when working with learning disabled college students. She suggested emphasis on the following ideas: realistic information about employment trends and current and future job markets; accurate information about educational and certification requirements; examples of coping strategies and adaptations used by successful disabled persons working in various careers; and decision-making based on aptitude, interests, and ability.

Swan (1982*) viewed career goal-setting as very important for enhancing learning disabled students' motivation to complete college. Because of their ignorance of what they could accomplish in the job world, he viewed career planning as an essential component of the learning disabilities college program. In his program at California State University, Long Beach, Swan includes a component on values clarification, and personality and interests assessment. In addition, students in the program sample the world of work through participation in volunteer programs and parttime jobs.

Doonan and Boxer (1983) found that approximately one-third of the participants in the learning disabilities program at Curry College felt that

---

*Swan, RJ. *A counseling model for promoting academic success of learning disabled students at the university level.* Unpublished manuscript, California State University at Long Beach, 1982.

certain occupations were not possible for them to pursue because they were learning disabled. Some of these occupations were: medicine, politics, flight industry, secretarial areas, science-related industries, and areas requiring writing such as journalism. These students' restrictive career perceptions underscore the importance of career counseling.

14

Preparing the Learning Disabled
Student for College

Many learning disabled students who plan to go to college graduate from high school unprepared to meet the demands of college. They frequently have insufficient knowledge of content subjects, are underachieving in the basic skills, do not understand their learning disability, have difficulty with interpersonal relationships, and have a fragmented understanding of what college is about.

If learning disabled college-bound students are to succeed in college, they must be adequately prepared by high school teachers and counselors. Without a concerted effort by high school teachers and counselors, learning disabled high school students will find a schism between themselves and non–learning-disabled college students that may be too wide to be crossed.

In this chapter, we offer a number of recommendations for teaching and counseling high school students to prepare them better for college. We believe these recommendations will help learning disabled high school students make better use of assistance offered by learning disabilities college programs, and function in college independently at an earlier date.

TEACHING RECOMMENDATIONS

As Quinlan pointed out on July 16, 1982, high school teachers must help their learning disabled students acquire an education that is consistent with their abilities. The students must be involved in a developmental curriculum that is commensurate with their age and level of intellectual ability, rather than in a curriculum reduced to the level of their basic skills deficiency. As Quinlan emphasized, high school teachers must teach learning disabled students at the levels of their ability and not at levels of their disability. The following recommendations will help high school personnel deliver more effective instruction for learning disabled college-bound students.

Enroll learning disabled students in college preparatory courses. Frequently learning disabled students are placed in courses that do not provide them with the prerequisite knowledge they need to enter college courses in English, mathematics, physical science, and social science. Consequently, when they arrive at college, they know fewer facts and generalizations from these subject areas than their non–learning-disabled peers who have completed a college preparatory curriculum.

Provide content area instruction by specialists. Some learning disabled high school students receive their content area instruction from learning disabilities teachers who are not certified or trained in specific content areas. This staffing pattern reduces both in quantity and quality the information presented to learning disabled students in the important subject areas of English, mathematics, physical science, and social science. It is important that college-bound learning disabled students receive their content area instruction from teachers who are trained specialists in the areas in which they are teaching.

Provide assignments similar to those required in college. When learning disabled high school graduates enter colleges and enroll in courses, they will be required to read novels, write book reviews, make oral reports, write research or term papers, and complete other independent projects. Learning disabled students should have extensive instruction and practice in doing these assignments.

Teach students to read textbooks effectively. Students must be taught textbook reading strategies to improve comprehension and retention of information they read. Robinson (1974) recommends that high school students use the SQ3R strategy for reading textual material in the social sciences. Each character in the mnemonic device SQ3R stands for one of the steps in the strategy: *S*urvey, *Q*uestion, *R*ead, *R*ecite, *R*eview. Spache (1963) recommends the PQRST strategy for reading textual materials in the physical sciences. Each letter in the strategy stands for one of the steps in the reading process: *P*review, *Q*uestion, *R*ead, *S*tudy, *T*est. Subject area teachers who teach these strategies will find their students reap the benefits of improved achievement.

Teach graphic aids. Textbook authors use a variety of graphic aids to explain the technical writing that appears in their textbooks. These graphic aids are used to explain text discourse in a manner that is more readily done with graphic aids than with words. The most common graphic aids found in textbooks are graphs, tables, charts, diagrams, flowcharts, and maps. High school subject area teachers should help learning disabled college-bound students develop the skills to understand these graphic aids. No one is more qualified to explain to learning disabled students how the graphic aids in a textbook should be interpreted than the subject area teacher teaching from that textbook.

Teach students the major study skills.   Learning disabled college-bound high school students should be taught the following study skills:

1.   Location skills used to locate information in a variety of information sources found in the classroom and libraries.
2.   Organization skills used to organize information for taking notes, preparing outlines, and writing various types of papers.
3.   Interpretation skills used to interpret information obtained from different sources as well as to interpret different styles of writing.
4.   Retention skills used to selectively remember important terms, concepts, and information.
5.   Test taking skills used to take different types of tests to demonstrate acquired information or skills.
6.   Rate skills used to differentiate reading rate according to purposes for reading.

Teach students how to organize study time and space.   College students have a considerable amount of unscheduled time they must learn how to use wisely in order to complete study activities and yet have time for fun activities. Learning disabled high school students need to be taught how to organize their study efforts for maximum efficiency. One way to help learning disabled students organize time and study areas is to pair them with a study partner. The study partner must be a student who has good organizational skills and who can help the learning disabled student monitor and complete assignments.

Teach students to function independently.   Many learning disabled students receive excessive assistance from siblings, teachers, and parents. This along with highly structured and supportive learning disabilities high school programs often combine to produce overly dependent learning disabled students. High school personnel must carefully evaluate the assistance they provide to learning disabled students to ensure they are not taking away students' needs for self-sufficiency. College-bound learning disabled students must be given increased responsibility for meeting requirements and resolving their own problems. The most successful learning disabled college students are those who can take responsibility for their own lives.

Teach students how to use auxiliary aids. When learning disabled students get to college, they probably will use auxiliary aids such as tape recorders to record lecture notes, taped textbooks for reading assignments, typewriters for writing assignments, and hand calculators for mathematics assignments. These auxiliary aids help learning disabled students compensate for their learning difficulties. Students will be able to use these auxiliary aids more successfully if they are exposed to them in high school.

Teach students how to take SAT and ACT tests. Students should understand that while cutoff scores from the SAT and ACT tests may not be used to determine whether or not they will be admitted to a college, they will be used to assess what they know and to assign them to classes. Coaching learning disabled students for admission examinations may help them achieve scores that more accurately reflect their potential and the knowledge they have acquired, rather than reflecting their learning disability. As part of the coaching, the students should be made aware of the alternative conditions under which they may take these tests.

Develop written language skills. Program directors reported that the two areas of severest underachievement among learning disabled students entering college were composition and spelling. During high school years, learning disabled students should be required to take four to six units of English instead of the typical three to four. The focus should be to teach them to write clearly and precisely with appropriate capitalization, punctuation, grammar, and spelling. Instruction in spelling should concentrate upon the 3000 high utility writing words that make up 99 percent of all the words used in written correspondence. Students should be taught to rely upon dictionaries to help them spell the other words they will need in their compositions. Daily writing activities are a must for learning disabled college-bound students.

Provide intensive vocabulary instruction. Learning disabled students often have a more restricted vocabulary than their non–learning-disabled peers. This is a problem for learning disabled students when they are trying to communicate their ideas through writing, understand a professor's presentation, or comprehend an author's ideas expressed in a textbook. Vocabulary development needs to be emphasized in all content area classes and not just relegated to the English teacher. All high school teachers should teach learning disabled students the meanings of key words in their subject areas using concrete activities. Learning disabled students find it very difficult to expand their vocabularies solely by looking words up in the dictionary or discussing definitions.

Continue to emphasize basic skills development. The higher the level of basic skills possessed by learning disabled students when entering college, the greater their likelihood of success in college. High school personnel should provide basic skills remediation to learning disabled students not only during each academic year, but summers as well. This is necessary to obtain the maximum amount of achievement for learning disabled college-bound students.

COUNSELING RECOMMENDATIONS

Learning disabled college-bound students are often inadequately prepared to go to college because they have not been appropriately counseled in high school. They frequently have no idea of what college is about or how difficult college is. Often they have an overinflated estimate of their ability, fuzzy career goals, and no understanding of their learning disability. The following recommendations will assist high school guidance counselors in helping learning disabled college-bound students get ready for college.

Give students a realistic assessment of their potential for college. Learning disabled students will often take basic rather than college preparatory classes in high school. Frequently they attend classes with students who have no intention of going on to college. As a result, learning disabled students often develop inflated perceptions of their cognitive ability, which are reinforced by inflated academic grades. These inflated perceptions and grades can lead some learning disabled students errone-ously to believe they can succeed in college.

High school counselors must assess the intellectual abilities of all learning disabled students who declare they are interested in pursuing a college education. Counselors can do this by administering individual intelligence tests, talking with the students' teachers, and comparing students with declared college interests to those learning disabled students who have gone on to college and have succeeded. With interpretations of this information by counselors, learning disabled students will be able to make realistic assessments of their potential for college.

Provide students with information about learning disabilities college programs. In the appendix we list a number of directories that list colleges that have programs for learning disabled students. We suggest that high school counselors acquire these directories and then send a form letter to each program they are interested in requesting brochures, catalogs, application forms, and other appropriate materials that will give information about the college learning disabilities program. The materials should be filed in folders by the name of the college. These materials should be reviewed with learning disabled students interested in going to college. Counselors should refer to Chapter 16 for ideas on how to evaluate programs.

Help students make application to learning disabilities programs. Presently there are few comprehensive learning disabilities college programs. While more programs are becoming available each year, there are still an insufficient number of programs available to serve the number of qualified learning disabled students who want to go to college. Because of this shortage, program directors recommend that students make their applications during their Junior year. High school counselors must help learning disabled sophomores think about college majors and become familiar with college programs for learning disabled students. During the Junior year, high school counselors must help learning disabled students assemble all information and complete all forms that are part of the application process.

Help students get ready for college admission interview. Most college programs for learning disabled students require applicants to visit the college and participate in an interview before they are officially admitted. For most learning disabled students, these are their first formal interviews and as a result there is the possibility that they will not present themselves in a representative manner. High school counselors should help learning disabled students prepare for admission interviews. An effective technique is to conduct mock interviews in which counselors ask students questions similar to those they will be asked during admission interviews. Here are the important questions directors of college learning disabilities programs ask students.*

Why do you want to attend college?
Why do you want to attend this college?
What do your parents think about your going to college?
What would you like to major in?

---

*Personal communications from K. Chandler, June 9, 1982; B. Cordoni, June 21, 1982; R. Nash, June 17, 1982; P. Quinlan, July 16, 1982; D. Saddler, July 14, 1982; S. Vogel, June 16, 1982; and G. Webb, July 15, 1982.

What are your plans after college?
What kind of a person are you?
What kind of learning disability do you have?
How does your learning disability affect you?
What are your academic strengths and weaknesses?
What kinds of things are easy for you to learn? Which are difficult?
What things have helped you to learn in the past?
What help do you need from our program to make it in college?
Are you prepared to spend extra time and effort to make it in college?

Develop interpersonal skills.   Learning disabled students often have difficulty making it in college because they lack the interpersonal skills to relate to other college students. Non–learning-disabled students often see them as loud, immature, unsure of themselves, and manipulative. These learning disabled students can benefit from rap sessions with guidance counselors and non–learning-disabled students. The discussions can focus upon the specific problems the learning disability high school students are having, the ways they are perceived by other students, types of problems the guidance counselor knows learning disabilities students will experience in college, and information on the dynamics of interpersonal relationships. Directors of college learning disabilities programs told us that few of their students dropped out of college because of academic problems. Most dropped out because of their inability to adjust to the social environment of college. Many of these dropouts may not have occurred if these students developed good interpersonal skills before entering college.

Provide career advisement.   Learning disabled students frequently have vague notions of what they want to do with their lives. Because of their limited knowledge and experience, they are aware of relatively few career options. They typically identify careers that are glamorous, associated with large amounts of money, or with which a close family member is involved. Learning disabled college-bound students need to be exposed to many career options through job fairs, field visits, and career classes. They also need to participate in testing programs to assess their aptitudes and interests. All this needs to begin in the Freshman year of high school so students know by their Junior year whether their career aspirations require a college education.

Help students understand their learning disabilities.   Learning disabled students who do not understand the effects of their learning disabilities are going to find college difficult. While they do not need a technical explanation of their learning disability, they must understand what they can and cannot do and what makes it easier for them to succeed. For example, students should know if they typically need more time to take examinations, if they need their textbooks on tape in order to read and understand them, if they need to use calculators for basic math operations, or if they need typewriters to prepare legible manuscripts. High school guidance counselors can help learning disabled students achieve a nontechnical but practical understanding of their learning disabilities that will help the students request appropriate services when they get to college.

15

Teaching Learning Disabled
Students in the College Classroom

For learning disabled students to succeed in college their professors must be sensitive to their needs. Professors must know how to adjust instruction for the unique learning styles of learning disabled students. The U.S. Department of Education sponsored a three-year demonstration project at Central Washington University designated as Higher Education for Learning Disabled Students (HELDS project). This project was designed to provide comprehensive services to learning disabled students. A major component of project HELDS was to train college professors to work with learning disabled students. The focus of the faculty training component was to teach professors how to modify their instructional techniques to provide an academic environment conducive to learning for these students. The faculty members participated in monthly training programs with experts in the field of learning disabilities. They also met with learning disabled students enrolled at Central Washington University. At these meetings the learning disabled students expressed their viewpoints and shared their experiences.

After the training sessions were completed, participating faculty members wrote manuscripts in which they described instructional modifications for their courses. These modifications were designed to increase achievement by learning disabled students. These manuscripts were published as seventeen booklets in 1982. The booklets are:

Bicchieri, M, (Professor of Anthropology). *Introducing anthropology to everyone*
Bilyeu, EE, (Professor of Spanish). *Practice makes perfect*
Briggs, KA, (Associate Professor of Health Education). *Accommodating students with learning disabilities in college health education*
Brunner, G, (Assistant Professor of Technology and Industrial Education). *Teaching electricity with learning disabled students*

Dugmore, WO, (Associate Professor of Counseling). *A humanistic approach to the teaching of courtship and marriage*

Garrett, R, (Associate Professor of Communication). *Implications and applications for speech communication*

Goodey, D, (Associate Professor of Psychology). *Psychology of adjustment and the learning disabled student*

Habib, HS, (Professor of Chemistry). *Suggestions for modifications in the teaching of general chemistry to accommodate learning disabled students*

Herum, J, (Professor of English). *A college professor as a reluctant learner: Facing up to the learning disabled*

Kramer, Z, (Professor of History). *Cleo and the learning disabled*

McKernan, CC, (Assistant Director Academic Skills Center). *Spelling is as spelling does*

Reinhardtsen, J, (Assistant Professor of Education). *Special education courses for the learning disabled*

Reynolds, RR, (Assistant Professor of Mass Media). *The learning disabled student in a television and radio announcing course*

Sands, CJM, (Assistant Professor of Anthropology). *Bare bones, An introduction to physical anthropology*

Sessions, F, (Professor of Sociology). *Learning disabled students in the behavioral and social sciences*

Utzinger, J, (Professor of Philosophy). *Logic for everyone*

Zink, KE, (Professor of English). *Let me try to make it clearer*

The professors participating in project HELDS presented many strategies for effectively teaching learning disabled students in college classrooms. We reviewed these booklets to identify those instructional strategies applicable across all disciplines. College professors interested in specific booklets should contact: HELDS Project, Myrtle Snyder, Director HELDS, Educational Opportunities Program, Central Washington University, Ellensburg, WA 98926; (509) 963-2131.

TEACHING STRATEGIES

Project participants uniformly agreed that instructional modifications made for learning disabled students must not alter the content and standards of courses. As one professor commented, slowing down or watering down a course would deprive the rest of the class of learning opportunities. Project participants also agreed that teaching strategies that help learning disabled students help the other students in their courses as well. The premise of the HELDS project was that strategies used to help learning disabled students achieve would help all students without hindering or interfering with the normal progress of courses.

Specific teaching strategies to assist learning disabled students gleaned from this project are described in the remainder of this chapter.

Provide a detailed syllabus. A syllabus should include: general objectives of the course, requirements and expectations, specific topics to be covered, and a calendar that specifies due dates for assignments and dates for all tests. The syllabus should be read aloud to the entire class to ensure that learning disabled students understand what the course is about and what is expected of them. The syllabus should be designed to ensure that learning disabled students will easily be able to determine where they've been, what is expected of them, and where they are going. By having the syllabus available before the course begins, learning disabled students can arrange a time table to pace themselves in the course, map out study strategies in advance, and make arrangements for special help such as taped textbooks.

Choose textbooks carefully. Professors should choose textbooks that: are carefully organized, have questions that provide purposes for reading, progress from simple to complex ideas, include many sub-headings, provide graphics to explain the text, have chapter summaries, and contain glossaries, indexes, and appendexes.

Explain how to use textbook aids. Professors should teach learning disabled students how to use the: table of contents, index, glossary, chapter summaries, pictures with captions, graphs, tables, and techniques of emphasis such as bold type and italics.

Assign advance readings. Students should be required to begin reading assignments in their textbooks at least one week before the topic is due for class presentation. This preexposure will enable learning disabled students to more fully understand classroom lectures and discussions.

Provide handouts. Professors should distribute handouts to expand on course topics and to augment material in the text. Handouts should not contain too much information on each page. Important information and key points should be italicized, capitalized or underlined. Professors should use numbers or letters to indicate organization. Since dittos often make blurry copies that are difficult for learning disabled students to read, where feasible, photocopies should be used.

Develop a positive student–teacher relationship. The progress of learning disabled students in their college courses is facilitated when they establish good relationships with their professors. Achievement is enhanced when professors demonstrate interest in and take time to understand the problems of learning disabled students. Most learning disabled students are shy and therefore reluctant to contact their professors. Professors must take the initiative and make appointments with the students.

Use a multisensory approach. Professors should use a variety of visual and auditory methods to present information. Visual methods include textbooks, transparencies, charts, flash cards, films, overhead projection, and the chalk board. Auditory methods include lectures, tapes, and records. Learning disabled students are often helped by seeing and hearing things simultaneously. As professors lecture they should write on the chalk board, use slides, use an overhead projector, and/or use video tapes or films. Before each class session professors should ask themselves if what they are presenting can be presented in more than one way. If it can, they should do so.

Use role-playing techniques. Role-playing techniques can be used to provide learning disabled students with opportunities to learn concepts through concrete experiences. Role-playing also provides learning disabled students with important opportunities to socially interact with their fellow students.

Review material. To help learning disabled students to retain information professors should review material. It is important to begin each class session with a brief review of the material previously covered. At the end of each class, professors should recap what was covered that day.

Provide repetition. All concepts, terms, and information introduced in a course should be reviewed as frequently as possible thereafter. Oral and written exercises should be used for reinforcement.

Gain the students' attention. Many learning disabled students have difficulty focusing or sustaining attention. Professors should use voice inflection, eye contact, and body gesturing to highlight significant points. Professors can attract students' attention by moving about the room as they teach. Colored chalk or colored overlays are also helpful. When a professor notices that a learning disabled student is easily distracted, the professor should seat the student near the front of the room and frequently call upon the student to answer questions.

Ask questions. Answering questions allows learning disabled students to hear themselves produce versions of what the professor has presented. Answers also allow professors to assess how well students understand the material.

Provide opportunities for previewing. Previewing course material prepares learning disabled students to anticipate the points to be made by a professor during a presentation. Previewing also helps students get organized for taking notes.

Personalize information. Attempt to personalize the material by relating it to learning disabled students' own experiences. This makes the information more meaningful to the students and enhances its retention. Professors should relate the material they present to events that the students may have read about, heard about, or watched on television.

Give frequent quizzes. Weekly quizzes provide continuous feedback for learning disabled students. Their performance on quizzes reveals areas where students need to study more. The results also help professors identify areas needing review.

Teach mnemonics. Learning disabled students have difficulty remembering information. Professors should use mnemonics to help the students remember important information. For example, the sentence, "Lambs can dance merrily," can be used to help learning disabled students remember roman numeral equivalents (fifty equals *L*ambs, one hundred equals *C*an, five hundred equals *D*ance, one thousand equals *M*errily).

Provide lecture outlines. To help learning disabled students take notes, outlines should be made available to them before lectures are delivered. The outline should be typed with ample space provided for students to take notes. Occasionally, to help students evaluate their note taking, professors should provide completed notes for a lecture.

Help students follow lectures. Professors must organize their lectures to enable learning disabled students to follow them. To accomplish this, professors can use a three-step approach: tell the students what you are going to tell them, tell it to them, and tell them what you told them.

Encourage small group discussions. Learning disabled students frequently benefit from participating in small group discussions where the group members seek to answer questions supplied by the professor. This allows the students to work through the material a second time and to be aware of alternative interpretations of the material.

Teach initial concepts deductively. In a deductive approach to teaching concepts, the basic concepts are simply stated at the beginning and then illustrated with examples. The straightforward expository format of deductive reasoning makes it an effective technique for introducing concepts to learning disabled students.

Use concrete presentations. Learning disabled students are generally most comfortable with new information when it is illustrated with examples that establish contact with concrete reality and observational experience. Professors should provide as many concrete examples and practical applications as is feasible and consonant with the materials and objectives of their lesson.

Use the chalkboard. Professors should record information on the chalkboard that reinforces what they present orally during a lecture. This provides opportunities for learning disabled students to see the correct spelling of terms and also improves the accuracy and efficiency of note taking.

Clarify points. Learning disabled students frequently do not grasp points the first time they are presented. Professors should clarify important concepts by presenting them a second time using different wording and new examples.

Clarify relationships. When presenting new information professors should clarify its relationship to previously presented information. Analogies are particularly useful for this purpose.

Extend time limits. Learning disabled students often work slowly. They must be given time limits for assignments that correspond to their working rates. It is particularly important to give these students more time for major writing assignments.

Control level of language. Most learning disabled students have difficulty understanding complex spoken language. Professors should avoid using unnecessarily long sentences and esoteric words. Concepts and information pertaining to a course should be presented simply and concisely.

Teach definitions and terms carefully. Professors must write definitions on the chalkboard and read and explain them to the students. The definitions should be reviewed at every opportunity. Definitions should not be paraphrased from one occasion to the next, but kept as uniform as possible. To help learning disabled students understand a textbook chapter, a list of key terms should be distributed and reviewed by the professor prior to assigning a chapter.

16

Selecting a Learning Disabilities College Program

An increasing number of colleges and universities are opening their doors to learning disabled students. Some are doing so primarily because of their commitment to learning disabled students, others to be in compliance with Section 504, and still others primarily because learning disabled students represent a new source of tuition dollars during a period of declining college enrollments.

Parents and professionals who help learning disabled students select colleges and universities must carefully examine any that claim to offer programs for these students. While some colleges provide the full range of services that constitute a special program for learning disabled students, many that claim to, do not. This latter group provides little more than those services traditionally available to all college students. These services are inadequate for learning disabled college students who, to succeed in college, need the full range of comprehensive services presented in the earlier chapters of this book.

To begin the process of college selection, parents and professionals should refer to Appendix 2 of this book and order the resources that will enable them to identify colleges with learning disabilities programs in the geographical area(s) of interest to the student. When a number of colleges have been identified, write them for information on their learning disabilities programs. Table 16-1 provides a sample letter for requesting program information. We recommend this letter be prepared by the student to demonstrate his or her initiative and interest in the program.

Once the information has been received, use the Evaluation of Learning Disabilities College Programs checklist presented in Table 16-2. This checklist contains a series of questions that must be answered about any learning disabilities college program before having a student apply to the program and college. The checklist is arranged so a number of learning

Table 16-1 Sample Letter for Requesting Program Information

Student's Street Address
City, State   Zip
Current Date

Name of Learning Disabilities Program
Name of College or University
Address
City, State   Zip

Dear Director: *(use name if known)*

I am a student with a learning disability and am completing my *(Junior, Senior)* year at *(name of high school)*. I expect to graduate *(date)* and then go on to college.

Please send me any information about your learning disabilities program, admission forms, a college or university catalog, and any other specific information that will assist me in learning about your program.

Thank you for any assistance you are able to give me.

Sincerely,

Name of Student

---

disabilities college programs can be compared. To answer some of the questions, it may be necessary to contact the program director, assistant director, or director of admissions.

The checklist enables the user to compare programs on two dimensions, total number of services, and specific types of services. To determine the total number of services provided by a program, simply add up the number of *yes* responses in its column and compare total scores. By comparing the number of *yes* responses each college receives, the user can make a quantitative comparison between programs.

To determine if the services one believes to be most important for one's students are provided by a program, one should locate the questions that refer to these services and see if a *yes* response is present. This procedure allows the user to make a qualitative judgment about a program.

Once the quantitative and qualitative judgments have been made, the user can put the program results in rank order in terms of suitability for a student. This results in a preferential order that the student may use for applying to colleges and visiting programs on college campuses.

When the choice of programs has been narrowed to a few colleges, we recommend that the student and parent(s) each visit college campus to speak with program staff concerning the questions in Table 16-2, see the campus and talk with students participating in the program. Table 16-3

Table 16-2 Evaluation of Learning Disabilities College Programs Checklist

Directions: Write the name of each college program to be evaluated at the top of the column under Names of Programs. Review the information you have obtained and answer each question. Write YES or NO as the answer for each question. Do this for each program.

Names of Programs

Questions to Ask About Learning Disabilities College Programs

1. Are there special admissions procedures?

2. Are diagnostic tests used to plan students' programs?

3. Is an individual educational program (IEP) developed for each student?

4. Are program staff members trained in learning disabilities?

5. Do college faculty members receive formal training to accommodate learning disabled students in their classrooms?

6. Are special advisors available?

7. Is reduced course load an option?

8. Is substitution for required courses permitted?

9. Is remediation in basic skills provided?

10. Is course tutoring provided by trained tutors?

11. Are taped textbooks available?

12. Are students permitted to use tape recorders to tape class sessions?

13. Are notetakers available?

14. Can arrangements be made to take course examinations in alternative ways?

15. Do program staff members serve as advocates for students?

16. Is individual and/or group counseling available?

17. Are special courses and/or special sections of courses available?

18. Are the students fully mainstreamed into college life?

Table 16-3 Sample Letter Requesting Campus Visit

Student's Street Address
City, State   Zip
Current Date

Name of Learning Disabilities Program
Name of College or University
Address
City, State   Zip

Dear Director: *(use name if known)*

    I have read the information you sent me about the Learning Disabilities Program at *(name of college or university)*.

    I would like to visit your program and to talk to someone on your staff, see the campus, and talk to some students in the program. Please arrange a visit for me on any of the following dates: *(list two or three available dates)*.

    I look forward to hearing from you about a date when I may visit your campus.

Sincerely,

Name of Student

provides a sample letter requesting a campus visit. This letter should also be prepared by the student. Table 16-4 provides questions that can be asked of students who have participated or are currently participating in the program to assess the students' impressions of the effectiveness of the learning disabilities college program and the appropriateness of the college.

Table 16-4 Questions to Ask Students in Learning Disabilities Program

Do program staff members understand your problems?

Does the program provide you with the types of help you need to make it in college?

Does the program provide you with the materials and equipment you need to do well in your courses?

Do faculty members make accommodations to help you succeed in their classes?

Are you accepted by students outside the program?

Do you like the other students in the program?

Is there someone to go to when things are really going poorly?

Do you believe the college really wants to have this program?

Do you believe the program helps you achieve in college?

Would you recommend this program and college to a learning disabled student?

References

Anderson, CJ (Ed). *1981–1982 Fact book for academic administrators*. Washington, DC: American Council on Education, 1981

Astin, AW, Hemond, MK, & Richardson, GT. *The American Freshman: National Norms for Fall 1982*. Los Angeles, CA: University of California at Los Angeles, Higher Education Research Institute, 1982

Bailey, CW. Adapting to the revolution of equal opportunity for the handicapped (No. 25). In MR Redden (Ed), *New directions for higher education: Assuring access for the handicapped*, Vol. 7 (No. 1). San Francisco, CA: Jossey-Bass, 1979, pp. 81–111

Bannatyne, A. Diagnosis: A note on recategorization of the WISC scaled scores. *Journal of Learning Disabilities*, 1974, 7, 272–273

Barbaro, F. The learning disabled college student: Some considerations in setting objectives. *Journal of Learning Disabilities*, 1982, 15, 599–603

Bireley, M, & Manley, E. The learning disabled college student in a college environment: A report of Wright State University's program. *Journal of Learning Disabilities*, 1980, 13, 12–15

Blalock, G, & Dixon, N. Improving prospects for the college-bound learning disabled. *Topics in Learning and Learning Disabilities*, 1982, 2, 69–78

Brown, D. *Counseling and accommodating the student with learning disabilities* (*ERIC Document Reproduction Service No. ED 214 338). Washington, DC: President's Committee on Employment of the Handicapped, 1982

Chesler, BM. *A talking mouth speaks about learning disabled college students*. Sacramento, CA: "A Song," 1980

Cordoni, B. Assisting dyslexic college students: An experimental program design at a university. *Bulletin of the Orton Society*, 1979, 29, 263–268 (a)

Cordoni, B. Davis–Typing keys to the remediation of reading and spelling

---

*ERIC is the Educational Resource Information Center. To obtain ERIC documents, write ERIC Document Reproduction Service, Computer Microfilm International Corporation (CMIC), 3030 N. Fairfax Drive, Suite 200, Arlington, Virginia 22201; or call (703) 841-1212.

difficulties. *Journal of Learning Disabilities*, 1979, *12*, 500 (b)

Cordoni, BK. College options for the learning disabled. *Learning Disabilities: An Audio Journal for Continuing Education*, 1980, *4*

Cordoni, BK. Personal adjustment: The psycho-social aspects of learning disabilities. In MR Schmidt, & HZ Sprandel (Eds), *New directions for student services: Helping the learning disabled student* (No. 18). San Francisco, CA: Jossey-Bass, 1982, pp. 39–47

Cordoni, BK. Services for college dyslexics. In RN Malatesha, & PG Aaron (Eds), *Reading disorders: Varieties and treatment*, in HA Whitaker (series Ed), Perspectives in neurolinguistics, neuropsychology, and psycholinguistics. New York, NY: Academic Press, 1982, pp. 435–447

Cordoni, BK, O'Donnell, JP, Ramaniah, NV, Kurtz, J, & Rosenshein, K. Wechsler Adult Intelligence score patterns for learning disabled young adults. *Journal of Learning Disabilities*, 1981, *14*, 404–407

Cronin, ME, & Gerber, PJ. Preparing the learning disabled adolescent for adulthood. *Topics in Learning and Learning Disabilities*, 1982, *2*, 55–68.

Cruickshank, WM, Bentzen, FA, Ratzeburg, FH, & Tannhauser, MT. *A teaching method for brain-injured and hyperactive children*. Syracuse, NY: Syracuse University Press, 1961

Deshler, DD, & Graham, S. Tape recording educational materials for secondary handicapped students. *Teaching Exceptional Children*, 1980, *13*, 52–54

Doonan, M, & Boxer, ST. Survey of the participants in the Program of Assistance in Learning at Curry College, Milton, Massachusetts, 1971–1980. In WM Cruickshank, & E Tash (Eds), *Academics and beyond: The best of ACLD*, Vol. 4. Syracuse, NY: Syracuse University Press, 1983, pp. 146–156

Edles, N. Higher education enrollment nearing peak. In BJ Chandler (Ed), *Standard education almanac. 1981–1982* (14th ed). Chicago, IL: Marquis Academic Media, 1981, pp. 144–145

Fielding, PM (Ed). *A national directory of four year colleges, two year colleges, and post high school training programs for young people with learning disabilities* (4th ed). Tulsa, OK: Partners in Publishing, 1981

Guerin, GR, & Maier, AS. *Informal assessment in education*. Palo Alto, CA: Mayfield, 1983

Guthrie, RC. Understanding the "legal technicalities" of federal regulations. In MR Redden (Ed), *New directions for higher education: Assuring access for the handicapped* (No. 25). San Francisco, CA: Jossey-Bass, 1979, pp. 69–79

Hanson, GS. The administrative challenge: Compliance by wit and reason. In MR Redden (Ed), *New directions for higher education: Assuring access for the handicapped* (No. 25). San Francisco, CA: Jossey-Bass, 1979, pp. 53–59

Hartman, RC. *Strategies for advising disabled students for postsecondary education*. Washington, DC: Higher Education and the Handicapped Resource Center, 1981

Hartman, RC, & Redden, MR. *Measuring student progress in the classroom*. Washington, DC: Higher Education and the Handicapped Resource Center, 1982

Hensen, JW, Kent, L, & Richardson, GT. *The handicapped student in America's colleges: A longitudinal analysis. Part 2: National norms for disabled and nondisabled college freshmen: 1978 and 1980* (ERIC Document Reproduction

Service No. ED 215 626). Los Angeles, CA: University of California at Los Angeles, Higher Education Research Institute, 1981

Hessler, GL. *Use and interpretation of the Woodcock-Johnson Psycho-Educational Battery.* Hingham, MA: Teaching Resources, 1982

Item analysis of Slosson Intelligence Test for Children and Adults. East Aurora, NY: Slosson Educational Publications, 1978

Jastram, PS. The faculty role: New responsibilities for program access. In MR Redden (Ed), *New Directions for higher education: Assuring access for the handicapped* (No. 25). San Francisco, CA: Jossey-Bass, 1979, pp. 11–22

Johnson, SW, &. Morasky, RL. *Learning disabilities* (2nd ed). Boston, MA: Allyn and Bacon, 1980

Knowles, BS, &. Knowles, PS. A model for identifying learning disabilities in college-bound students. *Journal of Learning Disabilities*, 1983, *16*, 39–42

Lawrence, JK, Kent, L, &. Henson, JW. *The handicapped student in America's colleges: A longitudinal analysis.* Part 1: *Disabled 1978 college Freshmen* (ERIC Document Reproduction Service No. ED 215 625). Los Angeles, CA: University of California at Los Angeles, Higher Education Research Institute

Lawrence, JK, Kent, L, &. Henson, JW. *The handicapped student in America's colleges: A longitudinal analysis.* Part 3: *Disabled 1978 college freshmen three years later.* Los Angeles, CA: University of California at Los Angeles, Higher Education Research Institute, 1982

Leslie, L. Financing colleges and universities. In HW Mitzel (Ed), *Encyclopedia of educational research* (5th ed). New York, NY: The Free Press, 1982, pp. 691–695

Lutwak, N, &. Fine, E. Counter-therapeutic styles when counseling the learning disabled college student. *Journal of College Student Personnel*, 1983, *24*, 320–324

Nash, RT. Project Success: A college support program for LD students. In *Their World.* New York, NY: Foundation for Children with Learning Disabilities, 1983, pp. 86–87

Ostertag, BA, Baker, RE, Howard, RF, &. Best, L. Learning disabled programs in California community colleges. *Journal of Learning Disabilities*, 1982, *15*, 535–538

Pascal, GR, &. Suttell, BJ. *The Bender Gestalt Test.* New York, NY: Grune &. Stratton, 1951

Redden, MR, Levering, C, &. DiQuinzio, D. *Recruitment, admissions and handicapped students.* Washington, DC: The American Association of Collegiate Registrars and Admissions Officers and The American Council on Education, 1978

Robinson, FP.. Study skills for superior students in secondary school. In LE Hafner (Ed), *Improving reading in middle and secondary schools* (2nd ed). New York, NY: Macmillan, 1974, pp. 185–191

Rogan, LL, &. Hartman, LD. *A follow-up study of learning disabled children as adults. Final report* (ERIC Document Reproduction Service No. ED 163 728). Washington, DC: Bureau of Education for the Handicapped, 1976

Rosenthal, I, Fine, E, &. deVight, R. Delivering services to the learning disabled: A holistic approach. In L Wilson (Ed), *New directions for college learning assistance: Helping special student groups* (No. 7). San Francisco, CA: Jossey-Bass, 1982, pp. 47–57

Ross, SK, & O'Brien, MB. *504 and admissions: Making the law work for the applicant and the college* (ERIC Document Reproduction Service No. ED 206 355). Minneapolis, MN: St. Mary's Junior College, 1981

Sedita, J. *Section 504: Help for the learning disabled college student* (ERIC Document Reproduction Service No. ED 207 412). Prides Crossing, MA: Landmark School, 1980

Semmel, DS. *A manual on individualized education programs.* Bloomington, IN: Indiana University, Center for Innovation in Teaching the Handicapped, 1979

Smith, CR. *Learning disabilities.* Boston, MA: Little Brown, 1983

Southeastern Community College v. Davis. *Supreme Court Reporter,* 1978, *78,* 1–15

Spache, GD. *Toward better reading.* Champaign, IL: Garrard, 1963

Stowitschek, JJ, Gable, RA, & Hendrickson, JM. *Instructional materials for exceptional children.* Rockville, MD: Aspen Systems, 1980

Ugland, R, & Duane, G. *Serving students with specific learning disabilities in higher education—A demonstration project at three Minnesota community colleges* (ERIC Document Reproduction Service No. ED 135 434). Bloomington, MN: Normandale Community College, 1976

Vocational Committee Survey. *Association for Children and Adults with Learning Disabilities Newsbriefs,* 1982, pp. 20–33

Vogel, SA. On developing LD college programs. *Journal of Learning Disabilities,* 1982, *15,* 518–528

Vogel, SA, & Adelman, P. Personnel development: College and university programs designed for learning disabled adults. *Illinois Council for Exceptional Children Quarterly,* 1981, *1,* 12–18

Vogel, SA, & Moran, MR. Written language disorders in learning disabled students: A preliminary report. In WM Cruickshank, & JW Lerner (Eds), *Coming of age: The best of ACLD,* Vol. 3. Syracuse, NY: Syracuse University Press, 1982, pp. 211–225

Vogel, SA, & Sattler, JL. *The college student with a learning disability: A handbook for college and university admissions officers, faculty, and administration.* Palatine, IL: Illinois Council for Developmental Disabilities, 1981

Webb, GM. The neurologically impaired youth goes to college. In RE Weber (Ed), *Handbook on learning disabilities.* Englewood Cliffs, NJ: Prentice-Hall, 1974, pp. 243–257

White, WJ, Alley, GR, Deshler, DD, Schumaker, JB, Warner, MM, & Clark, FL. Are there learning disabilities after high school? *Exceptional Children,* 1982, *49,* 273–274

Wiederholt, JL, & McNutt, G. Evaluating materials for handicapped adolescents. *Journal of Learning Disabilities,* 1977, *10,* 132–140

Women are increasing lead in enrollment on campus (UPI, Washington). *The New York Times,* March 21, 1983, p. A-13

Worcester, LH. *The Canadian Franco-American learning disabled student at the University of Maine at Orono* (ERIC Document Reproduction Service No. ED 204 881). Orono, ME: University of Maine at Orono, 1981

Worden, PE, Malmgren, IG, & Gabourie, P. Memory for stories in learning disabled adults. *Journal of Learning Disabilities,* 1982, *15,* 145–152

Worden, PE, & Nakamura, GV. Story comprehension and recall in learning-disabled versus normal college students. *Journal of Educational Psychology,* 1982, *74,* 633–641

Bibliography

Abrams, HG, & Abrams, RH. Legal obligations toward the post-secondary learning disabled student. *Wayne Law Review*, 1981, *27*, 1476–1499

Aiello, B. Adults, too, can be disabled learners. *New York Times Summer Survey of Education*, August 22, 1982, p. 24

Bacigalupo, M. Identification and accommodation of the college qualified learning disabled student. In SH Simon (Ed), *The accessible institution of higher education: Opportunity, challenge, and response* (ERIC Document Reproduction Service No. ED 216 487). Ames, IO: Association on Handicapped Student Service Programs in Postsecondary Education, 1981, pp. 171–175

Barsch, J. Community college: New opportunities for the LD student. *Academic Therapy*, 1980, *15*, 467–470

Blackburn, JC, & Iovacchini, EV. Student service responsibilities of institutions to learning disabled students. *College and University*, 1981, *57*, 208–217

Blalock, JW. Persistent problems and concerns of young adults with learning disabilities. In W Cruickshank & A Silver (Eds), *Bridges to tomorrow—The best of ACLD*, Vol. 2. Syracuse, NY: Syracuse University Press, 1981, pp. 35–55

Brown, D. Learning despite learning disabilities. In MR Schmidt, & HZ Sprandel (Eds), *New directions for student services: Helping the learning-disabled student* (No. 18). San Francisco, CA: Jossey-Bass, 1982, pp. 13–25

Cordoni, B. College programs for LD students. *Perceptions*, 1980, *3*, 1, 8

Cordoni, B. A directory of college LD services. *Journal of Learning Disabilities*, 1982, *15*, 529–534 (a)

Cordoni, BK. Postsecondary education: Where do we go from here? *Journal of Learning Disabilities*, 1982, *15*, 265–266 (b)

Cordoni, BK, & Snyder, MK. A comparison of learning disabled college students' achievements from WRAT and PIAT grade, standard and test scores. *Psychology in the Schools*, 1981, *18*, 28–34

Davis, VI. *Including the language learning disabled student in the college English class* (ERIC Document Reproduction Service No. ED 114 283). Lubbock, TX: Texas Technological University, 1975

Dexter, BL. Helping learning disabled students prepare for college. *Journal of Learning Disabilities*, 1982, *15*, 344–346

Gajar, AH, Murphy, JP, & Hunt, FM. A university program for learning disabled students. *Reading Improvement*, 1982, *19*, 282–288

Gelo, F. Higher education for the LD student. *Academic Therapy*, 1976, *11*, 349–355

Geyer, N, & Hartman, RC. *Fact sheet: The learning disabled adult and postsecondary education.* Washington, DC: HEATH/Closer Look Resource Center, 1981

Goodman, L, & Mann, L. *Learning disabilities in the secondary school.* New York, NY: Grune & Stratton, 1976

Gray, R. Serving adults with presumed learning disabilities—Some considerations. *Journal of Developmental and Remedial Education*, 1981, 4, 3–5, 33

Guildroy, J. The learning disabled college applicant. *The College Board Review*, 1981, *No. 120*, 28–30

Hartman, RC, & Krulurch, MT. *Learning Disabled Adults in Postsecondary Education.* Washington, DC: Higher Education and the Handicapped Resource Center, August, 1983.

Hastings, S, & Given, B. *Preparing the LD student for college.* Audiotape presented at the 19th International Conference of the Association for Children and Adults with Learning Disabilities. Washington, DC, 1983

Kahn, MS. Learning problems of the secondary and junior college learning disabled student: Suggested remedies. *Journal of Learning Disabilities*, 1980, *13*, 455–449

King, WL. Student services' response to learning-disabled students. In MR Schmidt, & HZ Sprandel (Eds), *New directions for student services: Helping the learning-disabled student* (No. 18). San Francisco, CA: Jossey-Bass, 1982, pp. 49–58

Leech, MM. Support services for the learning disabled on a limited budget. In SH Simon (Ed), *The accessible institution of higher education: Opportunity, challenge, and response* (ERIC Document Reproduction Service No. ED 216 487). Ames, IO: Association on Handicapped Student Service Programs in Postsecondary Education, 1981, pp. 176–181

Mangrum, CT, & Strichart, SS. College possibilities for the learning disabled: Part I. *Learning Disabilities*, 1983, 2, 57–68

Mangrum, CT, & Strichart, SS. College possibilities for the learning disabled: Part II. *Learning Disabilities*, 1983, 2, 69–81

Marsh, GE, Gearheart, CK, & Gearheart, BR. *The learning disabled adolescent.* Saint Louis, MO: CV Mosby, 1978

Miller, CD, McKinley, DL, & Ryan, M. College students: Learning disabilities and services. *The Personnel and Guidance Journal*, 1979, *58*, 154–158

Moorehead, S, Meeth, D, & Simpson, V. *A guide for college-bound learning disabled students.* Worthington, OH: Ohio Department of Education (undated)

Mosby, RJ. Secondary and college LD bypass strategies. *Academic Therapy*, 1981, *16*, 597–610

Moss, JR, & Fox, DL. *College-level programs for the learning disabled.* Tulsa, OK: Partners in Publishing, 1980

Nayman, RL. College learning assistance services and the learning-disabled college student. In MR Schmidt, & HZ Sprandel (Eds), *New directions for student* services: Helping the learning-disabled student (No. 18). San Francisco, CA: Jossey-Bass, 1982, pp. 69–85

Nelson, G. *A proposed system for developing individualized education programs for learning disabled adults at Vancouver Community College, King Edward Campus* (ERIC Document Reproduction Service No. ED 158 521). Paper presented at the World Congress on Future Special Education, Stirling, Scotland, 1978

Rogers, JC. Current clinical concepts of dyslexia in college students. In MR Schmidt, &. HZ Sprandel (Eds), *New directions for student services: Helping the learning-disabled student* (No. 18). San Francisco, CA: Jossey-Bass, 1982, pp. 27–38

Salter, MM. Beyond high school. In *Their World*, New York, NY: Foundation for Children with Learning Disabilities, 1983, pp. 82–83

Schmidt, MR. Academic adjustments and the faculty role in working with learning-disabled students. In MR Schmidt, &. HZ Sprandel (Eds), *New directions for student services: Helping the learning-disabled student* (No. 18). San Francisco, CA: Jossey-Bass, 1982, pp. 59–67

Schmidt, MR, &. Sprandel, HZ. Concluding remarks. In MR Schmidt and HZ Sprandel (Eds), *New directions for student services: Helping the learning-disabled student* (No. 18). San Francisco, CA: Jossey-Bass, 1982, pp. 87–91 (a)

Schmidt, MR, &. Sprandel, HZ. Sources for additional assistance: Literature and organizations. In MR Schmidt and HZ Sprandel (Eds), *New directions for student services: Helping the learning-disabled student* (No. 18). San Francisco, CA: Jossey-Bass, 1982, pp. 93–101 (b)

Schoolfield, WR. Limitations of the college entry LD model. *Academic Therapy*, 1978, *13*, 423–431

Siegel, D. Help for learning disabled college students. *American Education*, 1979, *15*, 17–21

Smith, LM. *The college student with a disability: A faculty handbook.* Washington, DC: The President's Committee on Employment of the Handicapped, 1981

Spalding, NV. *Learning about learning disabled college students* (ERIC Document Reproduction Service No. ED 198 857). Paper presented at the 4th Annual Institute for Directors of College Learning Centers, Berkeley, CA, 1980

Sprandel, HZ. Issues in providing services for the learning disabled on campus. In MR Schmidt and HZ Sprandel (Eds), *New directions for student services: Helping the learning-disabled student* (No. 18). San Francisco, CA: Jossey-Bass, 1982, pp. 39–47

Stalcup, RJ, &. Freeman, MA. Serving the learning disabled student in the community college. *Community College Frontiers*, 1980, *8*, 36–38

Swan, RJ. Reflections on a first year of a pilot program for learning disabled adults. *Journal for Special Educators*, 1982, *18*, 64–68.

Vaillancourt, B. *A special project for the development of assessment and educational programming techniques serving the adult basic education student with learning disabilities* (ERIC Document Reproduction Service No. ED 193 433). Springfield, IL: Illinois State Office of Education, 1979

Vandivier, PL, &. Vandivier, SS. The latent learner in college. *Improving College and University Teaching*, 1978, *26*, 211–212

Washington, MH. *A comprehensive approach to assessing and remediating learning disabilities in learning disabled college students* (ERIC Document Reproduction Service No. ED 218 839). Highland Heights, KY: Northern Kentucky University, 1981

Weiner, ES. Transition to college for LD students. *Academic Therapy,* 1975–1976, *11,* 199–203

Weller, C, & Strawser, S. Detecting learning disabilities in the college-aged student. *Learning Disability Quarterly,* 1980, *3,* 87–89

Wiig, E, & Fleischmann, N. Prepositional phrases, pronominalization, reflexivization, and relativization in the language of learning disabled college students. *Journal of Learning Disabilities,* 1980, *13,* 45–50

Winslow, R. College for the learning disabled. *New York Times Magazine,* February 21, 1982, pp. 80; 87; 90–91

Appendixes

Appendix   1
College Learning Disabilities Programs
Visited by the Authors of this Book

Curtis Blake Center
American International College
1000 State Street
Springfield, MA   01109
(413)   737-7000

Learning Opportunities Program
Barat College
700 E. Westleigh Road
Lake Forest, IL   60045
(312)   234-3000

Program of Assistance in Learning
Curry College
Milton, MA   02186
(617)   333-0500

Ben D. Caudle Special Learning Center
College of the Ozarks
Clarkesville, AR
(501)   754-3034

Specific Learning Disability Program
Erskine College
Due West, SC   29639
(803)   379-8867

Project Achieve
Southern Illinois University
Carbondale, IL   62901
(618)   453-2595

Project Success
University of Wisconsin—Oshkosh
Oshkosh, WI   54901
(414)   424-1032

Appendix 2
Directories of College Programs
for Learning Disabled Students

A guide to post-secondary educational opportunities for the learning disabled.

> DM Ridenour and J Johnston
> Time Out to Enjoy, Inc.
> 76 Lake Street—Suite 100
> Oak Park, Illinois   60301
> Publication date: 1981

A national directory of four year colleges, two year colleges and post high school training programs for young people with learning disabilities (4th ed).

> PM Fielding
> Partners in Publishing
> Tulsa, Oklahoma
> Publication date: 1981

Colleges/universities that accept students with learning disabilities.

> Association for Children and Adults with Learning Disabilities
> 4156 Library Road
> Pittsburgh, Pennsylvania   15234
> Publication date: Undated

Guide to College Programs for Learning Disabled Students.

> National Association of College Admissions Counselors
> 9333 Lawler Avenue, Suite 500
> Skokie, Illinois   60077
> Publication date: Undated

Listing of services for the postsecondary LD adult.

> Academic Therapy Publications
> 20 Commercial Boulevard
> Novato, California   94947
> Publication date: 1980

What do you do after high school?

> R Skyer and G Skyer
> Skyer Consultation Center, Inc.
> Rockaway Park, New York   11694
> Publication date: 1982

What's available for the learning disabled college student in Florida.
> MC Beech and L Smiley
> Florida Federation, Coucil for Learning Disabilities
> Publication date: 1982

Appendix 3
Organizations and Associations that Provide Services and Information to Learning Disabled Adolescents and Adults

Association for Children and Adults with Learning Disabilities (ACLD)

4156 Library Road
Pittsburgh, PA   15234
(412)   341-1515

ACLD has a number of state offices. These include:

Alabama ACLD
P.O. Box 11588
Montgomery, AL   36111

Arizona ACLD
P.O. Box 15525
Phoenix, AZ   85060
(602)   840-3192

Arkansas ACLD
P.O. Box 7316
Little Rock, AK   72217

Connecticut ACLD
20 Raymond Road
West Hartford, CT   06107
(203)   236-3953

Illinois ACLD
P.O. Box A-3239
Chicago, IL   60690
(312)   939-3513

Iowa ACLD
P.O. Box 2298
Des Moines, IA   54310
(515)   277-5383

Kansas ACLD
P.O. Box 4424
Topeka, KS   66604

Mississippi ACLD
P.O. Box 9387
Jackson, MS   39206
(601)   982-2812

New Hampshire ACLD
P.O. Box 3377
Manchester, NH   03103
(603)   669-8534

New Jersey ACLD
P.O. Box 249
Convent Station, NJ   07961
(201)   539-4644

Ohio ACLD
4601 N. High Street
Columbus, OH   42134
(614)   267-7040

Vermont ACLD
9 Heaton Street
Montpelier, VT   05602
(802)   223-5480

Association of Learning Disabled Adults

P.O. Box 9722
Friendship Station
Washington, DC   20016

Association on Handicapped Student Service Programs in Post Secondary Education

> P.O. Box 886
> Ames, IA   50010

Council for Exceptional Children (CEC)

> 1920 Association Drive
> Reston, VA   22091

Council for Learning Disabilities

> Department of Special Education
> University of Louisville
> Louisville, KY   40292

Foundation for Children with Learning Disabilities

> 99 Park Avenue
> New York, NY   10016
> (212)   687-7211

Friends of the Sensorially Deprived, Inc.

> P.O. Box 186
> Belmont, MA   02178
> (617)   484-0340

Georgia Organization for Adults with Learning Disabilities, Inc.

> 475 Burgundy Court
> Stone Mountain, GA   30087
> (404)   498-1606

Information Center for Individuals with Disabilities

> 20 Park Plaza, Room 330
> Boston, MA   02116
> (617)   727-5540

Launch, Inc.

> Department of Special Education
> East Texas State University
> Commerce, TX   75428
> (214)   886-5932

National Easter Seal Society

> 2023 W. Ogden Avenue
> Chicago, IL   60612
> (312)   243-8400

National Information Center for Handicapped Children and Youth

> P.O. Box 1492
> Washington, DC   20013

National Network of Learning Disabled Adults

> P.O. Box 3130
> Richardson, TX   75080

New York Association for the Learning Disabled

> 217 Lark Street
> Albany, NY   12210
> (518)   436-4633

Orton Dyslexia Society

> 724 York Road
> Baltimore, MD   21204
> (301)   296-0232

Parent Information Center

> P.O. Box 1422
> Concord, NH   03301
> (603)   224-7005

Perceptions, Inc.

> P.O. Box 142
> Millburn, NJ   07041

President's Committee on Employment of the Handicapped

> 1111 20th Street, NW
> Room 600
> Washington, DC   20036
> (202)   653-5010

The Puzzle People

> 122 Belvedere Drive
> Mill Valley, CA   94941
> (415)   388-4236

Time Out to Enjoy, Inc.

> 113 Garfield Street
> Oak Park, IL   60304
> (312)   383-9017

Appendix 4
Resource Guide: Special Services and Aids for Disabled Students Attending Postsecondary Education Institutions—1983

Today, postsecondary schools are increasingly meeting the national goal of providing equal educational opportunities for all Americans, by providing these opportunities to disabled persons. Prior to World War II, postsecondary educational opportunities for severely disabled persons were so limited that only the most highly motivated visually-, hearing-, or mobility-impaired individuals obtained a college education, and then only with extensive, longterm assistance from a few dedicated professionals—physicians, teachers, parents, and lay volunteers. Key events since then, the "GI Bill" combined with extensive efforts to rehabilitate and train disabled veterans, the development of State Vocational Rehabilitation programs for disabled adults, special education programs for disabled youngsters, and the passage of Section 504 of the Rehabilitation Act of 1973, have gradually produced a large-scale awareness of, and concern for, the moral and legal rights of disabled persons. Today, hundreds of schools, colleges, universities, and technical institutes enroll many thousands of academically qualified students with emotional/mental, learning, sensory, and mobility impairments ranging from the mildest to the most severe.

The increased awareness by college and university administrators and educators of the needs of disabled students stems in part from the U.S. Department of Education's implementing regulations for Section 504 of the Rehabilitation Act of 1973, as amended, which bans discrimination against disabled persons in programs and activities receiving Federal financial assistance. This statute requires postsecondary institutions receiving Federal financial assistance to review their policies and procedures and their employment practices, to eliminate discrimination against disabled persons, and also to review their facilities to make sure that the overall programs are accessible to disabled persons.

Many disabled students have, on their own initiative, discovered innovative ways of handling their disabilities and meeting the challenge of obtaining an education in college and university communities. Nevertheless, for those disabled students who may yet need special services, this Resource Guide may provide useful information on the many types of services that are available.

The first Section of this Resource Guide, entitled "Federal Programs," summarizes programs that provide special services and auxiliary aids to disabled postsecondary students. These programs provide services to the

This resource guide was prepared by: Handicapped Concerns Staff, United States Department of Education, Mary Switzer Building—Room 3124, Washington, DC 20202; (202) 245-0873; Chet Avery, Director. Reprinted as modified, by permission.

student through the postsecondary institutions, or directly to the disabled student on an individual, client-centered basis. Additional programs that may be of assistance to disabled college and university students are described in *Federal Assistance for Programs Serving the Handicapped*, which can be purchased from the US Government Printing Office (address: Superintendent of Documents, US Government Printing Office, Washington, DC 20402; telephone: (202) 783-3238. Cost is $7.50, send check or money order).

The second Section of this Resource Guide contains a listing of other organizations that provide services that may be of benefit to disabled students pursuing a postsecondary education.

Section I.   Federal Programs

Federal Programs Providing Special Services to Disabled Students Attending Postsecondary Educational Institutions

Special Services for Disadvantaged Students

Legislative authority: The Higher Education Act of 1965, as amended, Title IV, Subpart 4, Section 417.

Program description.   This program provides supportive and other services so that postsecondary students can remain in and graduate from postsecondary educational programs.

Services to disabled postsecondary students: Provides personal, career, and academic counseling; provides remedial and referral services; develops program and uses special curricula and instructional methods; helps students obtain adequate financial aid; provides auxiliary aids (readers, notetakers, interpreters, etc.) to physically disabled postsecondary students.

Campus contact person for disabled postsecondary students: Special Services Project Director, or Director of Grants Office, or Student Financial Aid Officer at the university, college, or community college. In addition to the Special Services Project Director, there may be a Coordinator of Disabled Student Services on the university, college, or community college campus.

Eligible student applicants: An individual with academic potential, meeting Special Services eligibility requirements, who needs remedial/ special services as a result of a physical disability.

Eligible recipients: Postsecondary educational institutions.

Appropriations: 610 awards, $63.9 million in fiscal year 1981; 640 awards, $60.7 million, 1982; 640 (noncompeting continuations) awards, $60.7 million, 1983.

Federal contact persons: Mr. Richard T. Sonnergren, Director, Division of Student Services, Office of Postsecondary Education, Room #3042 ROB-3, U.S. Department of Education, 400 Maryland Avenue, S.W., Washington, D.C. 20202; Telephone: (202)   426-8960.

Regional Postsecondary Education Programs for Deaf and Other Handicapped Persons

Legislative authority: Education of the Handicapped Act (PL 91-230), Section 625, 20 USC 1424a.

Program description: To develop and operate models of specially designed or modified programs of vocational-technical, postsecondary or adult education for deaf and other disabled persons.

Services to disabled students: Resources and services needed by disabled persons to assist in their successful integration into a nondisabled school population and regular educational program, by provision of an integrated, comprehensive range of services. These services are designed to enable disabled students to compete academically with nondisabled persons. Illustrative of resources, services, and activities that may be supported (in whole or in part):

Interpreters	Preparatory and orientation services
Tutors	Supplementary Learning
Notetakers	Experiences
Wheelchair Attendants	Instructional Media
Guidance Counselors	In-service training for teachers
Auditory Training	and other staff
Job placement and follow-up	Planning and Evaluation Activities

Federal funding under this Program shall *NOT* be used for payment of tuition or subsistence allowance, as well as cost of construction.

Campus contact person for disabled postsecondary students: Not applicable, since there are few model grants.

Eligible student applicants: Student benefits accrued if the student's college or university campus has a grant under this program.

Eligible recipients: Institutions of higher education, and other appropriate nonprofit educational agencies.

Appropriations: 18 new awards, $2,950,000, 1981; no new grant competition held—8 continuations awarded, $2,832,000, 1982; 12 continuations and 2 new deaf program awards, $2,832,000, 1983.

Vocational Education (Services for Disabled Students)

Legislative authority: Section 110(a) of Vocational Educational Act of 1963, as amended in 1976 (Regulations sections 104.303—"minimum percentages" and 104.311—"Federal share of expenditures" and "National Priority Programs" in Monday, October 3, 1977 edition of the *Federal Register*).

Program description: This program helps support, on a matching basis, the *additional* vocational services disabled persons need to succeed in Vocational Education Programs.

Services to disabled students: Provides the necessary modified vocational programs and/or supportive services required by disabled persons enrolled in vocational education at secondary, postsecondary, or adult levels.

Campus contact person for disabled postsecondary students: Dean or Director of Career/Vocational Programs.

Eligible student applicants: A disabled individual in an appropriate job preparation program (non-baccalaureate), who requires supportive services to successfully complete the program.

Eligible recipients: Awards are made through State Vocational Education Agencies to local education agencies, which grant funds to local secondary institutions, community colleges, and vocational-technical centers.

Appropriations: $61,208,273 in 1981, $58,773,694 in 1982, and $58,773,664.80 in 1983. Funds are allotted to the 50 states, District of Columbia, Territories, and Possessions by grants.

Federal contact person: Dr. LeRoy A. Cornelson, Director, Division of State Vocational Programs, Office of Vocational and Adult Education, Room #5640 ROB-3, U.S. Department of Education, 400 Maryland Avenue, S.W., Washington, D.C.   20202; Telephone   (202)   472-3440.

Cooperative Education Program

Legislative authority: Higher Education Act of 1965, as amended, Title VIII, Sections 802 and 803.

Program description: This program supports the planning and implementation of programs integrating periods of academic study with public or private employment, as well as training, research, and demonstration projects that are to be made available to all qualified students in all academic disciplines.

Services to disabled students: Projects are funded to provide work experiences related to academic discipline or career objectives. Individual services to disabled students are provided at the discretion of the postsecondary institution receiving the grant.

Campus contact person for disabled postsecondary students: Director, Cooperative Education Program on campus.

Eligible student applicants: Academically qualified students enrolled in an institution of higher education, other than by correspondence, in a degree program of not less than two years' duration, who carries at least half of the academic workload normally required of persons who are fulltime degree candidates.

Eligible recipients: Nonproprietary accredited two- or four-year postsecondary institutions, excluding purely vocational/technical programs.

Appropriations: 236 awards, $23 million, 1981; 197 awards, $14.4 million, 1982; 190 awards, $14.4 million, 1983.

Federal contact person: Dr. Morris Brown, Director, Division of Institutional and State Incentive Programs, Office of Postsecondary Education, #3053 ROB-3, U.S. Department of Education, 400 Maryland Avenue, S.W., Washington, D.C. 20202; Telephone (202) 472-5389.

College Work-Study Program

Legislative authority: The Higher Education Act of 1965, as amended, Title IV, Part C, Sections 441–447.

Program description: The College Work-Study Program (CWS) provides jobs for students who need financial aid and who must earn a part of their educational expenses.

Services to disabled students: Students employed through the College Work-Study Program can provide reader and notetaker services for visually-impaired students and students with manual disabilities. These students can, if trained, provide interpreter services for deaf students, and attendant services for mobility-impaired students.

Campus contact person for disabled postsecondary students: Campus Financial Aid Administrators.

Eligible student applicants: Graduate, undergraduate, and vocational students who are enrolled at least half-time as regular students in an eligible program at an approved postsecondary institution. The participating college or university may spend up to 10 percent of its CWS allocation of Federal funds to employ less than half-time students.

Eligible recipients: Postsecondary educational institutions.

Appropriations: 3,244 institutions, $550 million, 1981; 3,290, $528 million, 1982; 3,400, $590 million, 1983.

Federal contact person: Mr. Robert Coates, Chief, Campus and State Grants Branch, Division of Program Operations, Room #4642 ROB-3, U.S. Department of Education, 400 Maryland Avenue, S.W., Washington, D.C. 20202; Telephone: (202) 245-2320.

The Fund for the Improvement of Postsecondary Education (FIPSE)

Legislative authority: Title X of the Higher Education Act of 1965, as amended, 20 USC 1135.

Program description: Supports innovative (action oriented) model projects improving access to and quality of postsecondary education. The program is field-oriented; potential grant recipients let project officers know what areas and issues need attention in projects. Projects are funded for one, two, or three years.

Services to disabled students: FIPSE has supported many model projects improving access to and quality of postsecondary education for disabled students. For example, currently funding a community-based project to provide high quality interpreter services to local education institutions that enroll hearing-impaired students.

Campus contact person for disabled postsecondary students: Not applicable.

Eligible student applicants: Not applicable.

Eligible recipients: Any institution or organization that proposes to serve postsecondary students, colleges, and universities (broad applicant eligibility).

Appropriations: 180–190 (roughly half were continuations) awards, $13.5 million, 1981; 71 new grants, 111 renewals, $13.5 million, 1982; 60–70 new grants, 115 renewable, appropriations figure not available, 1983.

Federal contact person: Ms. Diana Hayman, Program Director, Fund for the Improvement of Postsecondary Education, Office of Postsecondary Education, Room #3100 ROB-3, U.S. Department of Education, 400 Maryland Avenue, S.W., Washington, D.C. 20202; Telephone: (202) 245-8091.

Educational Opportunity Centers

Legislative authority: The Higher Education Act of 1965, as amended, Title IV, Subpart 4, Section 417.

Program description: This program is designed to serve areas with major concentrations of low-income populations and to assist individuals who: may need information on financial and academic assistance; may need assistance in applying for admission to postsecondary institutions; and may need counseling, tutorial, and other necessary assistance while enrolled in a postsecondary program.

Services to disabled students: Collect and disseminate information regarding financial aid, provide counseling on career opportunities, assist in preparing applications for admission to institutions, provide tutorial assistance to students who are residents, and involve the community in the formulation of the application and operation of the center.

Campus contact person for disabled postsecondary students: For further information, write or call the Office of Postsecondary Education, Division of Student Services, US Department of Education, Washington, DC 20202; Telephone: (202) 426-8960.

Eligible student applicants: A student must live in a target area served by the Educational Opportunity Center. The individual must need the services offered by the Center, and be interested in pursuing a post-secondary education.

Eligible recipients: Institutions of higher education, public and private agencies and organizations, secondary schools, and secondary vocational schools.

Appropriations: 32 awards, $8.0 million, 1981; 33 awards, $7.8 million, 1982 and 1983.

State-Federal Vocational Rehabilitation Program

Legislative authority: Title I of PL 93-112, The Rehabilitation Act of 1973, as amended.

Program description: Under the basic support program, assistance to disabled persons is provided by State Vocational Rehabilitation Agencies. In some states, there are two Agencies: one serving blind persons only, and another for persons with any other disability. Title I of the Rehabilitation Act, as amended, provides for Federal financial assistance to States. Funds are allocated on a matching basis of 80 percent Federal and 20 percent State.

Services to disabled students: A wide range of services are available for eligible disabled persons. An individual need not be a student to apply.

*1. Evaluation
 2. Medical, surgical, and hospital care, and related therapy, to remove or reduce disability
 3. Prosthetic and orthotic devices
*4. Counseling, guidance, referral, and placement services
 5. Training services
 6. Services in comprehensive or specialized rehabilitation facilities
 7. Maintenance and transportation during the rehabilitation
 8. Tools, equipment, and licenses for work on a job or in establishing a small business
 9. Initial stock, supplies, and management services for small businesses, including acquisition of vending stands by the State Agency
 10. Reader services for blind persons, and interpreter services for deaf persons
 11. Recruitment and training services to provide new careers for disabled persons in the field of rehabilitation and other public service areas

12. Rehabilitation teaching services and orientation and mobility services for blind persons
13. Telecommunications, sensory, and other technological aids and devices
14. Services to families of disabled persons when the services will contribute to the rehabilitation of the client
15. Post-employment services, including follow-up and follow-along, to help disabled persons hold a job
16. Other goods and services to render a disabled individual employable

All items except those asterisked (*) may be subject to a test of a client's ability to pay, or to the use of similar benefits from another source before the expenditure of Agency funds.

Section II.   Other Programs

National Library Service for the Blind and Physically Handicapped

The National Library Service for the Blind and Physically Handicapped, Library of Congress, loans books and magazines on cassettes, discs, and in braille, to individuals who have problems reading because of visual or physical limitations, temporary or permanent. Books, playback equipment, headphones, and other aids are delivered by mail, postage-free. Eligibility for the program is determined by the inability to see well enough to read a conventional-print book, or to hold a book and turn pages. For information on the regional lending library for blind and physically disabled persons in your area, as well as other sources for obtaining brailled and recorded materials, please contact:

> Reference Section
> National Library Service for the Blind
>   and Physically Handicapped
> 1291 Taylor Street, N.W.
> Washington, D.C.   20542
> Telephone: (202)   287-5100

The Association of Handicapped Student Services Program in Postsecondary Education

The Association on Handicapped Student Services Programs in Postsecondary Education (AHSSPPE) consists primarily of members of special services programs and Section 504 campus coordinators, working in over 300 postsecondary schools in the United States, Puerto Rico, and Canada. The Association can provide an annotated bibliography notebook of special services and auxiliary aids, which will be updated periodically. This bibliography can be obtained at a cost of $8.50 for AHSSPPE members, and $11.00 for other interested persons.

Additionally, the Association has a network of consultants who can be contacted to provide expert information on the provision of special services and auxiliary aids for disabled students in postsecondary education. For further information, contact:

> Ms. Sherry Robinson, Chairperson
> Communications Committee, AHSSPPE
> 12000 Southwest 49th Street
> Portland, Oregon   47219
> Telephone: (503)   244-6111, extension #339

> or: Ms. Sharon Bonney
> President, AHSSPPE
> 2515 Channing Way
> Berkeley, California   94720
> Telephone: (415)   642-0518

Project HEATH Resource Center

Project HEATH (*Higher Education and the Handicapped*) is a national clearinghouse of information about support services for disabled students in postsecondary institutions in the United States. The Resource Center publishes a news bulletin three times per year; develops and disseminates fact sheets and packets of materials about topics of concern to disabled students, postsecondary administrators, campus support services providers, and advisors of disabled potential students; and publishes a Resource Directory. In addition, the Center can provide telephone consultation about higher education and disabled persons, Section 504 of the Rehabilitation Act of 1973, and auxiliary aids. To be placed on the Project HEATH Resource Center mailing list, contact:

> Ms. Rhona C. Hartman, Director
> Project HEATH Resource Center
> American Council on Education
> One Dupont Circle
> Washington, D.C.   20036
> Telephone: (202)   833-4707—voice, then TDD*

---

*TDD—Telecommunication Device for the Deaf.

The National Student Educational Fund and
The United States Student Association

The National Student Educational Fund (NSEF) and the United States Student Association (USSA) have launched a national student leadership training program, with the purpose of providing information to college students about issues affecting their lives, as well as leadership and skills building training. NSEF and USSA hopes to train students to be advocates for higher education, civil rights enforcement, and student consumer concerns. Funded through a large three-year grant from the Carnegie Corporation of New York, with small contributions from the Arca Foundation, and Youth Project, four field coordinators will be working with statewide student associations, campus, women's organizations, racial minority student groups, and disabled student organizations. The major focus of the Disabled Student Leadership Network Project is to build campus disabled student organizations around the country, and to help include them in the higher education decision-making process, through involvement in student government associations, as well as state and national student organizations.

> Contact Person: Mr. Gary Brickman
> NSEF—USSA
> 2000 "P" Street, N.W., Suite #305
> Washington, D.C.   20036
> Telephone: (202)   785-1856

Section 504 Regional Technical
Assistance Staff Directory (Figure 1)

Region I: *Connecticut, Maine, Massachusetts, New Hampshire, Rhode Island, Vermont*

Director (vacant)   (617)223-4624
Regional Technical Assistance Staff   (FTS*)223-4248
Technical Assistance Office   TDD (617)223-1111
U.S. Department of Education
Office for Civil Rights, Region I
140 Federal Street, 14th Floor
Boston, Massachusetts   02110

Region II: *New Jersey, New York, Puerto Rico, Virgin Islands*

Dr. Frank A. Dolan, Director   (212)264-2906

---

*FTS—Facet Telephone Service.

Regional Technical Assistance Staff   (FTS)264-2906
Technical Assistance Office   TDD (212)264-4880
U.S. Department of Education
Office for Civil Rights, Region II
26 Federal Plaza, Room #33-100
New York, New York   10007

Region III: *Delaware, District of Columbia, Maryland, Pennsylvania*
                 Virginia, West Virginia

Ms. Joan Williams, Director   (215)596-6092
Regional Technical Assistance Staff   (FTS)596-6092
Technical Assistance Office   TDD (215)596-6794
U.S. Department of Education
Office for Civil Rights, Region III
Gateway Building
3535 Market Street, P.O. Box 13716
Philadelphia, Pennsylvania   19101

Region IV: *Alabama, Florida, Georgia, Kentucky, Mississippi,*
                North Carolina, South Carolina, Tennessee

Mr. Douglas J. Lawton, Director   (404)221-2806
Regional Technical Assistance Staff   (FTS)221-2806
Technical Assistance Office   TDD (404)221-3322
U.S. Department of Education
Office for Civil Rights, Region IV
101 Marietta Tower, Room #2725
Atlanta, Georgia   30323

Region V: *Illinois, Indiana, Michigan, Minnesota, Ohio, Wisconsin*

Ms. Catherine R. Condon, Director   (312)886-3064
Regional Technical Assistance Staff   (FTS)886-3064
Technical Assistance Office   TDD (312)886-3065
U.S. Department of Education
Office for Civil Rights, Region V
300 South Wacker Drive, 8th Floor
Chicago, Illinois   60606

Region VI: *Arkansas, Louisiana, New Mexico, Oklahoma, Texas*

Mr. Ted Crim, Acting Director   (214)767-2479
Regional Technical Assistance Staff   (FTS)767-2479
Technical Assistance Office   TDD(214)767-6599

U.S. Department of Education
Office for Civil Rights, Region VI
1200 Main Tower, Room #1930
Dallas, Texas   75202

Region VII: *Iowa, Kansas, Missouri, Nebraska*

Mr. John Nigro, Director   (816)374-7264
Regional Technical Assistance Staff   (FTS)767-2479
U.S. Department of Education   TDD (816)374-5025
Office for Civil Rights, Region VII
324 East 11th Street, 24th Floor
Kansas City, Missouri   64106

Region VIII: *Colorado, Montana, North Dakota, South Dakota, Utah,*
Wyoming

Mr. Mike Lopez, Director   (303)837-5295
Regional Technical Assistance Staff   (FTS)837-5295
U.S. Department of Education   TDD (303)837-3417
Office for Civil Rights, Region VIII
Federal Office Building
1961 Stout Street, 13th Floor
Denver, Colorado   80294

Region IX: *Arizona, California, Hawaii, Nevada, Guam,*
Trust Territories of the Pacific Islands, American
Samoa, Wake Island

Mr. Robert Scott, Director   (415)556-7140
Regional Technical Assistance Staff   (FTS)556-7140
Technical Assistance Office   TDD (415)556-1933
U.S. Department of Education
Office for Civil Rights, Region IX
1275 Market Street
San Francisco, California   94103

Region X: *Alaska, Idaho, Oregon, Washington*

Mr. J. Terry Carney, Director   (206)442-2618
Regional Technical Assistance Staff   (FTS)399-2618
U.S. Department of Education   TDD (206)442-4542
Office for Civil Rights, Region X
2901 3rd Avenue
Seattle, Washington   98121

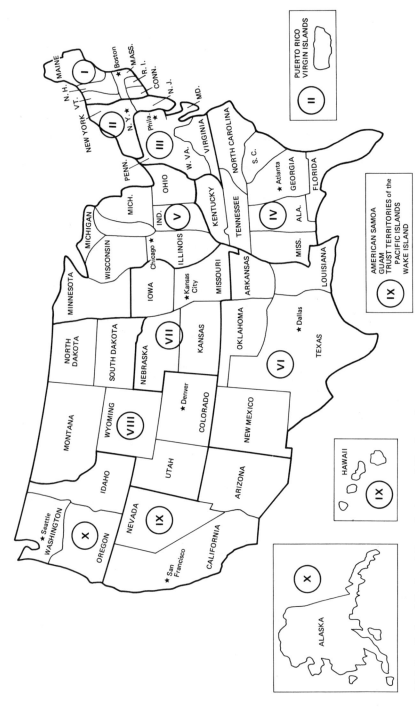

Fig. 1. Federal Regional Boundaries and Headquarters.

Index

a
b
c
4 d
5 e
6 f
7 g
8 h
9 i
8 0 j